BUILT for SPEED

BUILT for SPEED

JOHN GRIFFITH

Bounty
Books

Acknowledgments

The material in this book is based on a series of articles which the author contributed to *Motor Cycling* with *Scooter Weekly* to whom acknowledgment is due, together with thanks for their permission to reproduce the photographs.

First published in Great Britain in 1962
by Temple Press Books Ltd

This edition published in 2010 by Bounty Books,
a division of Octopus Publishing Group Ltd
Endeavour House,
189 Shaftesbury Avenue,
London WC2H 8JY
www.octopusbooks.co.uk

An Hachette UK Company
www.hachette.co.uk

Copyright © Octopus Publishing Group Ltd 2010

ISBN: 978-0-753719-90-9

A CIP catalogue record for this book is available from the British Library

Printed and bound in China

FOREWORD

Speed has always had an extraordinary fascination for the human race and in motorcyclists the attraction manifests itself on the various types of speed track where thousands of riders annually try their skill in one form of competition or another.

The machines they use are of diverse types. Some are the result of concentrated development work by great industrial concerns; others the outcome of patient work by a lone individual. Whether they are intended for grass-track, scramble, sprint, road-race or record attempt they all share one thing, they are 'Built for Speed'.

As many readers will know, that phrase formed the title of a series of articles originally published in *Motor Cycling* and for this volume I have selected a couple of dozen of these articles. They appear in no set order, for the series itself was intentionally varied.

If you aim to go fast yourself, take a close look at the other man's ideas—and if you think you spot a mistake, try to profit by it.

These machines, illustrated with detail-photographs and line drawings, are a cross-section of the motorcycling sporting movement, with representatives from Italy, Germany and Japan as well as London, Birmingham and Manchester. Many of the details given were first disclosed in *Motor Cycling* and up to the time of compiling this book, no other journal had ever recorded even the existence of the three special 'Works' Nortons, the rotary-valve single, the 'flat' single and the four-cylinder model, three machines that would undoubtedly have created a furore had they appeared on the race circuits. Much of the information on the four-cylinder M.V. models was supplied by race ace, John Surtees, whose ability as an engineer is second only to his skill as a rider.

Although all the machines described are the results of hours of research, rarely was I given a point-blank refusal to answer questions about them. The riders and owners generally were most helpful in supplying information which had taken them months, or years, to assemble. One or two were 'cagey', but they were those whose machines were currently striving to reach the top and who, justifiably, wanted to get there before helping others up! But in the main the details are here. If you need to know the valve timing for a successful record attempt read on—it's in this book!

JOHN GRIFFITH

CONTENTS

CONTENTS *continued*

The horizontal-engined machines that would have
carried the Factory Team in 1956

IN THE WINTER of 1954–55 came the news from Norton's that, in common with A.J.S.—the marque with whom they had battled for almost half a century on the race circuits of the world —they would no longer build 'works' racing machines or put official teams of riders in the field. Instead, racing development would be concentrated on the models sold to private owners.

This was a bombshell which changed the face of international racing. Less public, but equally drastic, were its effects at Norton's works at Bracebridge Street.

At the time of the fateful decision a team of new—dramatically new—racing models was being built at Norton's. Engines had been bench-tested and a prototype frame for the redesigned power unit had been made; in fact, the first machine was about to be taken to the M.I.R.A. track for test.

Rather sadly, I suspect, that great designer, team leader and tactician, the late Joe Craig, tucked his newest brainchild into the cellars. And 1955, which should have seen this machine on the test-track saw, instead, his retirement from Norton's. He moved to Holland and was tragically killed in March 1957 in a car accident.

In the cellars the machines languished until late 1959, when Norton's agreed to allow *Motor Cycling* to publish a story in the 'Built for Speed' series. Race development mechanic Jack Workman, with the goodwill of development engineer Doug Hele, painted and polished the relics until they looked presentable. The art department of Temple Press 'provided' the fuel tank (see leading illustration), as no tank was ever made for the original frame, but it had been intended to fit a deep one similar to those used on the last of the A.J.S. 'Porcupines'. It was not initially planned to fit streamlining.

The engine-room is undoubtedly the most interesting part of a racer, and this model is no exception. The unit is referred to at Norton's as the 'F' type— 'F' standing for flat (in posture not performance). It is, in fact, a revised 'Manx' engine lying on its face and built in unit with the gearbox.

The cambox and drive are virtually identical with the standard machinery of the year, but the cylinder head is very different. Finning appears to be much more extensive than usual and runs 'up and down' the head so that it lies parallel to the airflow. As was to be expected, finning is especially generous round the exhaust pipe/head joint which, on this type, is by a four-bolt-and-flange fixing instead of the threaded ring used on the other Norton racers. The separate head seen in the photographs is for the 350-c.c. engine; the only 500-c.c. type available when I went to the works was on the engine installed in the frame, but the two motors were more or less identical apart from swept volume.

One important feature, not immediately obvious, is that the engine runs 'backwards' because of the two-pinion internal primary-gear transmission. The axis of the Wellworthy 'Al-Fin' barrel is below the plane of the engine mainshaft at t.d.c. so that the engine is 'reverse *désaxé*'. Valve angle is standard 'Manx' (64°), as are the 2-in.-head KE965 inlet valve and 1·718-in.-head, sodium-filled, exhaust valve. Stem diameters are $\frac{5}{16}$-in. and ·048 in. respectively.

No separate crankpin is used in the crankshaft assembly. The drive-side mainshaft and bobweight are made in one piece with the crankpin itself and the timing-side shaft and bobweight are also integral, thus giving exceptional stiffness at ultra-high r.p.m.

The big-end, larger in diameter, both

IN BRIEF

Engine: Single-cylinder double o.h.c. in unit with 5-speed gearbox: 90-mm. bore × 78·4-mm. stroke = 499 c.c.; 78-mm. bore × 73-mm. stroke = 348 c.c.; c.r. (500) 10·6 : 1; power output (500) 50 b.h.p. (at rear wheel) at 7,600 r.p.m.

Ignition: Lucas coil and contact breaker.

Fuel: Light-alloy tank (size according to course).

Oil: 1 gal. carried in frame tube.

Wheels: Light-alloy rims carrying Avon racing tyres 3·00 in. × 19 in. at front, 3·50 in. × 19 in. at rear.

Brakes: 8-in.-diameter two-leading-shoe at front and rear, front centrifugally ventilated type.

The machine as it is today, showing the horizontal cylinder head finning.

Main moving parts. The two-piece crank-shaft assembly and the heavily webbed connecting rod.

inside and out, than the standard 'Manx' component, employs fifteen $\frac{7}{16}$-in. by $\frac{5}{8}$-in. caged rollers. Triple-caged roller-bearings support the drive side of the camshaft. On the timing side, back-to-back, angular-contact ball-bearings are fitted; these ensure the accurate crank-shaft end location so important with bevel drive to the camshafts. The two inner races can be adjusted by removal

and grinding, a lengthy but accurate process which eliminates shims.

The motor, when it was bench-tested, ran on 95-octane fuel fed through a special Amal G.P. carburetter. Of $1\frac{7}{16}$-in. bore at the slide, its inlet side body, mated by rubber hose to the inlet pipe, tapered to 1·406-in. bore at the head joint. An adapter carried on the carburetter base enabled the main jet to be carried in a near-vertical position, even though the body was 'horizontal'. The float chamber, not seen in the photographs, was to have been mounted on the front down-tubes of the frame. The little pipe on the carburetter body is a positive feed to the pilot jet.

Lucas coil ignition had been developed specially for the engine during all its experimental stages and was perfected for work at the peak of the power range. The contact-breaker assembly is carried in the casting at the base of the 'vertical' shaft; manual control of the timing is novel for a racer with coil ignition.

The oil pump is different from its predecessor in that a modified unit scavenges the cambox; the pipe can be

seen running from the bottom of the cambox back to the pump housing in the lower bevel box. A finned oil cooler is fitted to the return pipe from the oil-cooled exhaust valve, as was the practice in 1954.

Straight-cut gears take the power from engine to the five-speed gearbox. These are enclosed in a separate chamber outside of which the external flywheel and the clutch run in the cool air. Reference to the cross-sectional drawing of the unit will show this arrangement very clearly.

Three shafts are employed in the gearbox, a mainshaft and two layshafts, one above and below. Final drive is on the timing side of the unit, the box being of the cross-over type.

The frame of the machine, all of '531' Reynolds tubing, is notable, for it is a complete breakaway from the famous 'Featherbed'. The main member is a $4\frac{1}{2}$-in.-o.d. tube, which also acts as an oil reservoir. At its front end a steering head pivot-tube is Sifbronze-welded in place and, at the rear, plates are welded to it to form a box section which

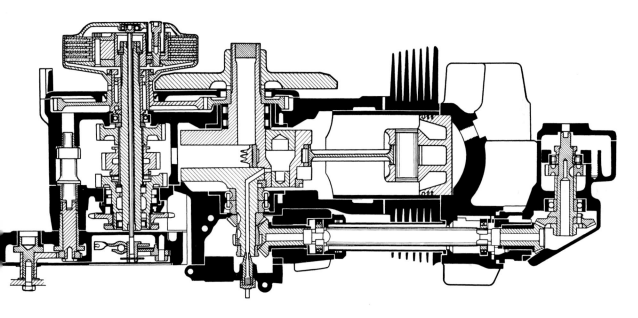

The engine and gearbox unit in horizontal section.

The gear-change pedal would normally lie between the footrest outrigger plate and the large polished alloy casting. The contact breaker hides behind the cover on the 'lower' bevel drive housing.

protrudes downward to carry the engine unit. From half way down the big main member, twin $\frac{7}{8}$-in.-section tubes run horizontally rearwards to terminate just above the tops of the rear spring units. Another pair of tubes extend from the base of the main member to mate up with the horizontal tubes at the rear; welded-in gusset plates provide fixing-points for the spring anchorages. For good measure, a third pair of tubes are welded in place between the big-tube base and horizontal tubes, just ahead of the seat nose; a piece of light plate, welded between the second pair, acts as a mudguard. Another pair of tubes are bolted between the cylinder and steering heads. The pivoting fork is carried by a large alloy plate on the flywheel side of the machine, which mates with two engine-frame bolts and one engine bolt just below the pivot. On the timing side the fork is supported by a very large alloy casting which mates with the same two engine-frame bolts and with a third point just behind the contact-breaker housing. This large casting encloses the foot change and clutch-operating mechanisms and shrouds from view the separate gearbox end-cover.

Unfortunately, this flat arrangement results in the wheelbase growing $1\frac{1}{2}$ in. longer than the orthodox 'Manx' with the normal 'Roadholder' front fork fitted. A type of trailing-link fork was

tested on standard-type models experimentally in 1954 but we cannot know if it would have been tried on this particular machine.

Both brakes are twin-leading-shoe type of 8-in. diameter; that at the front is of the centrifugally ventilated type

BELOW : Close-up of the engine showing how the light-alloy plate and casting provide a swinging fork pivot. Note the oil cooler near the cylinder head on return from exhaust valve.

ABOVE : *Head details: oil is fed to the tank via the cap just ahead of the steering-column.*

7

seen on the 1954 'works' models.

On the bench the '500' gave as much power at the rear wheel as the then 'works' team bike gave at the engine shaft, whether it would have been a better racer we shall never know!

Electron is used for all the major crank-case gearbox castings and for the primary gear-drive cover and contact-breaker housing. Head and barrel are retained by four through studs and nuts.

8

2 THE RICKMAN METISSE

A Triumph-B.S.A.-Norton hybrid of amazing potency

Each pair of rocker caps is bridged by a locking plate.

IN BRIEF

Engine: Parallel twin o.h.v.; 63-mm. bore by 80-mm. stroke = 498 c.c.; no c.r. or b.h.p. figures available.
Fuel tank: 2-gal. light-alloy.
Oil tank: 4-pt. steel.
Wheels: Steel rims with Dunlop tyres, 3·00 in. × 21 in. front, 4·00 in. × 19 in. rear.
Wheelbase: 56 in.

WHEN TWO RIDERS are consistently successful in scrambles events of national status, they can rightly be called stars even if their mounts are 'works' supplied. But when two riders of 'bitzas' consistently beat the best men and machines that Britain's factories can put in the field, that is *news*.

The Rickman brothers, D. J. (Don) and D. E. (Derek), well-known scramblers over the past few years and proprietors of a flourishing motorcycle business in Hampshire, decided in 1958 that, although their B.S.A. 'Gold Star' scrambles models were fast enough to enable them to keep up with the leaders at most meetings, they could, to their way of thinking, be faster.

During the winter, with help from G. H. ('Tiny') Camfield, a tuner of some repute in Triumph-twin circles, they built up a pair of specials, the now-famous Métisses.

The power plant is a Triumph 'Tiger 100' 500-c.c. twin. It has been hypnotized by 'Tiny' to give a wider power band than the standard tuned motor with, rather naturally, greater emphasis on the bottom end of the scale.

The bore and stroke are standard, the pistons have Wellworthy 'Lymalloy' rings and Champion N58R plugs are used. Carburation is by a pre-'monobloc' type 276 Amal instrument of $\frac{15}{16}$-in. bore with a remote float chamber which is carried on a bracket fixed to the oil tank. Ignition is by Lucas magneto.

The air cleaner is atop the oil tank, under the seat, and connected to the carburetter by a pipe passing through the tank. This arrangement keeps the cleaner free from mud, water and dust and yet allows efficient breathing for the motor.

The motor is installed in a B.S.A. 'Gold-Star' frame only slightly modified. Several spare lugs and brackets have been removed and keen-eyed onlookers can spot other minor changes. The engine plates are of aluminium alloy and are drilled and reamed so that all holes mate exactly with their counterparts in the engine, gearbox and frame. Working tolerance is negligible and none of the aircraft quality bolts has to be forced home; all are a 'nice push-fit'.

Chaincase and gearbox are also 'Gold Star'; indeed, the majority of the cycle parts are of this ancestry.

To make the rear wheel assembly stiffer, the standard rear spindle and ancillaries have been modified so that the 'eye' end of the swinging fork is clamped more rigidly; the pivot points, too, have been altered. At the front, a couple of strengthening rings have been shrunk on the head lug to support the bearing housing and a distance piece has been fitted to allow for the longer head stem of the 'Manx' Norton forks which are used. The forks have a standard Norton crown lug with integral handlebar clamps and the lower legs carry a 'Gold Star' front wheel.

The machine is completed by the curliest—I nearly wrote cutest—pair of exhaust pipes ever to grace a racer.

What of the name Métisse? Of the several alternatives which my French dictionary supplies, Derek and Don prefer 'mongrel'. Why they chose the feminine of the word is obscure.

The Triumph motor in the 'Gold Star' B.S.A. frame. Note the substantial light-alloy engine plates and the way in which the 'Gold Star' primary chain-case has been grafted on to the crankcase.

3 CHRIS VINCENT'S B.S.A. OUTFIT

Sole British '500' capable of challenging Munich twins in international sidecar racing

SUCCESS! Success so phenomenal as to be almost unbelievable has been achieved in the racing sidecar world by Chris Vincent and his low-slung B.S.A.-engined outfit.

In the 1960 T.T. the Vincent/B.S.A. pair performed admirably until they retired. Too well, perhaps, for it was then that idle gossip suggested that his motor was a '650'. Obviously the gossips had not given much thought to their speculation: Vincent, who works in B.S.A.'s experimental department (and whilst not actively encouraged by the factory, is certainly not discouraged), would scarcely have risked his racing career and his everyday livelihood by chancing such a stupid move.

What are the secrets of Vincent's success? There are several—although apart from certain aspects of engine internals they are not too secret. First, he is obviously a really first-class chariot-eer, that goes without saying; the outfit's handling must be beyond reproach, for the most skilled of workmen cannot do well without good tools—the outfit is fast!

There are two ways to make a machine go fast: develop a lot of power and to have as small head resistance as possible. Additionally, to get the most accelera-tion possible it is necessary to reduce weight to the bare minimum. Vincent has done all these things.

In the course of his work in the test shop at B.S.A. he obviously gains a lot of data. He told me that, although he does *not* develop his own engines at the factory, he does use all the data he learns there when incorporating modifi-cations in his own units. The 500-c.c. 'Shooting Star' design units look out-wardly standard, but it goes without saying that they are not. Each 500-c.c. engine he has differs from its counter-parts in slight details, so that effects of different alterations can be noted. All have modified porting; valve timing, diameters and lift are the subject of experiments and Chris refused to tell me more than that, or what compression ratio he employs. The valve angle is still standard and shell plain bearings are used for the big-ends. A plain timing-side and lipped roller drive-side mains

One Amal carburetter with two S.U. float chambers feeds the motor.

IN BRIEF

Engine: Parallel-twin o.h.v.; iron block; light-alloy head; 66-mm. bore × 72·6 mm. stroke = 497 c.c.; no other data available.

Transmission: B.S.A. four-speed gearbox with 'Gold Star' close ratios.

Fuel: 2-gal. alloy tank.

Oil: 7-pt. in frame down-tube and addi-tional reservoir.

Wheels: Light-alloy rims with Dunlop racing tyres 3·50 in. × 16 in. front; 4·00 in. × 16 in. rear; 3·50 in. × 12 in. sidecar; 7-in. rear broke; 'Gold Star' 190-mm. front brake.

Wheelbase: 56 in. approx.

Constructional details of forks with front wheel and streamlining removed.

are fitted plus a standard-type magneto. Castor-base oil is used and is carried in the frame front down-tube with an extra reservoir in front of the tube, across the shell.

Only one carburetter is used: this, a $\frac{15}{32}$-in. bore T.T. Amal, has two S.U. float chambers. (Sometimes a different choke size is tried.) Petrol is fed to these by electric pump from a tank carried beside the primary chain; for long races an extra $1\frac{1}{4}$-gal. tank is incorporated in the sidecar wing.

Transmission is via a standard B.S.A. gearbox with 'Gold Star' close-ratio internals.

So much for the works, but it is the rest of the machine that is so interesting. The chassis and frame are made in one piece and, without the rear swinging fork, they weigh only fifty pounds. The front forks are of leading-link pattern controlled by Girling hydraulically damped units and, with a head angle of about 63°, they give $\frac{3}{4}$ in. of trail. Wheelbase is about 56 in. and height to the top of the steering head is a mere two feet.

Especially interesting is the rear springing controlled by a rubber block and a rubber band on each side. Both block and band are in tension, *not* in torsion as is sometimes erroneously stated.

I have described the outfit as a '500', but Chris does have a '650' motor which can be installed in about forty-five minutes. Secrecy shrouds the internals of that engine also, but I was told it gives about ten per cent more power than the '500'—but it isn't used in 500-c.c. races!

Chris Vincent achieved even greater success with this outfit in 1962 when he won the I.O.M. Sidecar T.T.

**First machine to average
'the ton' for a day**

BY THE TIME you read these words, the 'world's fastest' 24-hour title may well have changed hands again. But if it changes hands a hundred times in as many days the name Velocette will stand out from all the rest, for to this English factory goes the credit of producing the machine that first exceeded 100 m.p.h. for a day—on March 18 to 19, 1961, at the Montlhéry track in France.

The machine was amazingly close to standard specification—in fact, I would go so far as to say that there are hundreds

---

IN BRIEF

Engine: Single-cylinder o.h.v.; light-alloy head; 86-mm. bore × 86-mm. stroke = 499 c.c.; c.r. 8·75 : 1; 39·8 b.h.p. at 5,900 r.p.m.
Transmission: Velocette gearbox with close ratios; 4 : 1 top.
Fuel: 3·7-gal. steel tank.
Oil: 4·5-pt. steel tank.
Wheels: Light-alloy rims with Dunlop racing tyres, 3·00 in. × 19 in. front, 3·50 in. × 19 in. rear.
Wheelbase: 53·75 in.
Rear suspension: Girling hydraulically damped spring units.

16

of 'Venom' riders in this country who could have converted (if that is the right word) their stock machines to put up just the same performance.

Let's get it straight. Unless otherwise stated everything mentioned in this article is *standard*, either as original equipment or as an optional extra.

Basically, the machine is the equivalent of the production 'Venom Clubman Vee-line' model. I say 'the equivalent' because the record-breaker was built in June 1960, before the announcement of the production machine, and was ready by August, having completed some 1,400 miles at over 'the ton' in practice runs.

The fairing fitted then, specially produced by the Amesbury factory of Mitchenall Bros., was—and still is—the prototype used for the 'Clubman Vee-line' models. Why didn't the factory fit a production version for the record attempt? The first maxim of successful record-breaking is to limit changes to the minimum.

The same reasoning applied to the retention of the old-type tank. Both these items had been proved to the hilt and

half a yard beyond, and to have carried out similar tests (far more rigorous than those needed for the equipment of normal machines) would only have caused unnecessary delay.

The engine was very carefully assembled and bench developed in June 1960. It had not been stripped, not even the head had been removed, until the record was in the bag. Then, of course, it had to be dismantled for measuring. That meant 1,400 miles of testing and 2,400 miles of record, all at over the '100' mark, without 'opening up'.

The motor is, of course, on now 'traditional' Velocette single-cylinder lines with a gear-driven high-camshaft and short—and so light—pushrods; an extension of the gear train drives the magneto, just astern of the barrel. This design, incidentally, was introduced (as a '250') almost thirty years ago!

The crankshaft assembly runs on Timken taper-roller main bearings; it has an Alpha big-end with eighteen caged $\frac{3}{16}$-in. × $\frac{9}{16}$-in. rollers.

A Nimonic 80 exhaust valve and

EN52 Silchrome inlet valve are controlled by hairpin springs. Valve timing is: inlet opens 55° before t.d.c., closes 65° after b.d.c.; exhaust opens 75° before b.d.c., closes 45° after t.d.c.—all checked with 0·030-in. tappet clearance. Running clearances used were: inlet 0·008 in., exhaust 0·010 in. (just for safety).

Manually controlled ignition is provided by a B.T.H. magneto and, for the record attempt, a non-standard Marchal plug (arranged by the French members of the *équipe*), was timed at 38° before t.d.c. on full advance.

The Amal GP carburetter, of $1\frac{3}{16}$-in. bore, has a 310 size main jet—which was too rich, but gave an ample safety margin, even at night. A $\frac{3}{4}$-in. packing piece, non-standard, was fitted between the cylinder head and carburetter, as it was found to be beneficial when bench tests were carried out. The $1\frac{3}{4}$-in.-bore exhaust pipe is 34 in. long and terminates in a KTT pattern megaphone, 12 in. long and with a $4\frac{1}{4}$-in. outlet.

Close-ratio gears are used (identical, incidentally, with those employed on the

The machine as it finished the run. Note the two sets of footrests to give the rider a change of position. Locking-wire was used on many nuts, including the rear brake anchor arm and carburetter base. The primary chain guard was changed, but the rear one retained.

17

The piston crown immediately after the head had been lifted at the end of the run.

last of the factory KTT racers), and sprocket sizes, front to rear, are 23t., 44t., 22t., 46t., which give a top gear ratio of precisely 4 : 1.

Dunlop racing tyres were used for the record attempt; actually, they provided some 'special' tyres for early tests, but these were found unnecessary. Brake-lining material was the same as is used on all big Velos, and the wheels had alloy racing rims. Only change to the frame was the *addition* of a centre stand, to help with quick wheel changes; even the sidecar lugs were left on!

As the model had no electrics (non-standard), the top fork covers, which have integral headlamp brackets, were dispensed with and rubber gaiters from a scrambler were fitted. The clip-on bars are non-standard, as are a set of pillion footrests fitted for an alternative riding position.

Non-standard also are the rubber-mounted oil tank and the float chamber carried on the front on it; non-standard is the open primary chain with two-pipe oiler from the engine's tank, and rubber-mounted guard which replaces the standard chaincase.

The rear chainguard is retained and the chain is lubricated by the oil-tank breather.

The record machine ran on 94-octane fuel and multi-grade (S.A.E. 20/40) engine oil. The oil tank was topped up at 4- or 5-hour intervals only to make good the drip to the chain; the oil wasn't changed. S.A.E. 50 lubricant was used in the gearbox.

I asked why 100 octane fuel was not used. Answer: It's not available in France.

Fuel consumption at a maintained 107 m.p.h. was 35–36 m.p.h. (13½ litres per hour) and maximum speed on the chosen gearing was a shade under 115 m.p.h.

5 LES ARCHER'S 500-c.c. NORTON SCRAMBLER

1960 edition of a famous home-built moto-cross model

Note the footrest fixing, with the exhaust pipe passing through the hanger portion, and the crankcase shield.

IN BRIEF

Engine: Single-cylinder o.h.c.; 79-mm. bore × 100-mm. stroke = 490 c.c.; c.r. 8·75 : 1; peak r.p.m., over 6,500; no b.h.p. figure available.

Ignition: Lucas manually controlled racing magneto.

Fuel: 1¾-gal. steel tank.

Oil: 1-gal. steel tank.

Wheels: Steel rims carrying Avon 'Gripster' tyres, 3·00 in. × 21 in. front, 4·00 in. × 19 in. rear.

Weight: 340 lb.

Wheelbase: 56 in.

BASED ON A long-stroke 'Manx' engine, L.R. (Les) Archer's 1960 scrambler was the latest of a line of specials built by Ron Hankins, Archer's experimental engineer.

Although at first glance the frame looks like a cross between a 'Featherbed' and a single-top-tube Norton, close inspection reveals that it is, in fact, very different from either. Built of 'A'-quality steel tubing; it has duplex downtubes which sweep under engine and gearbox and then upwards under the seat; these appear to be standard Norton parts, but are actually longer. A 'Manx' head-tube is employed with a single, fairly big, top tube.

Gusset plates carry the pivoting fork. This has been widened at the pivot end to clear the 4-in. rear tyre; it is controlled by Girling units. At the front standard ES2 forks are used with red-rubber gaiters, secured by Jubilee clips, to keep out dust.

Both hubs are of the 'Manx' conical type, with 8-in.-diameter brake drums. Naturally all air-scoops have been blanked off to keep the dust out, and the standard alloy rims have been replaced by steel ones.

The oil tank is made up in two parts, one atop the other. Oil is poured through the filler into the lower tank via a tube which runs well down inside. The engine draws its lubricant—castor-base—from this tank, but returns it to the top section, whence it runs back to the lower half via some half-dozen ⅛-in. bore tubes which are submerged at their lower ends in the main supply. This somewhat involved process prevents frothing; it also helps to cool the oil, almost a gallon of which is kept circulating.

"Standard long-stroke, 'Manx' bottom-end and barrel and 'Inter' head" —thus Ron summarily dismissed the engine. Feeling that he was not taking credit where it was due, I pressed him to enlarge on the subject.

True enough, the bottom end really *is* standard long-stroke 'Manx'. The barrel starts life with a 78·5-mm. bore so that it can be bored twice—to 79·0 and 79·62 mm.—without exceeding the 500-c.c. limit. Compression ratio is normally 8·75 : 1 but sometimes a plate is taken out to raise it to 9 or 9·2 : 1; it can happen that fuel claimed to be 98 octane on the Continent is sometimes not! As long as the motor revs over 6,000 Ron is happy. He tells me that it can be buzzed to 7,000 if necessary.

The head has been scooped out to take valves of 'Manx' head diameter, although stem diameter and guides are normal 'Inter'—there is 0·060 in. difference in head diameter between the two types I was told. The cambox, too, is 'Inter', although the cams have been modified to give more power in the lower revolutions range.

The carburetter is a modified 10TT9 Amal instrument of $1\frac{3}{32}$-in. to $1\frac{5}{32}$-in. bore, according to conditions. A great deal of work has been carried out in sealing the carburetter from dust; both float chamber and air slide are connected to the atmosphere by pipes connected to the air-cleaner box. The cleaner is really very special; with the cover removed, it looks like a window frame with four Vokes felt-and-wire filter elements as the panes. Ron smears the back wall of the cleaner with grease and then stipples it with a brush. The dust which does pass the filter is flung outward on to the grease which, after a meeting, is just like grinding-paste.

Transmission is by 'Manx' clutch and special gearbox. The internals employ the highest bottom gear that can be used with a kickstarter and a 'Manx' third gear.

The mainshaft is longer than standard so that the final-drive sprocket can be packed out to throw the chain clear of the tyre. Consequently the engine sprocket also has to be packed out. The primary drive is in a steel case and chain life is good. Rear chains last two or three meetings.

The front tank-fixing bracket, sandwich-type oil tank and rear chain guide plate.

Footrests are massive; each is fixed by three bolts—two to a bracket on the frame and the common throughbolt. An extra-hefty engine plate is used between head and frame top tube, this also acts as an engine steady.

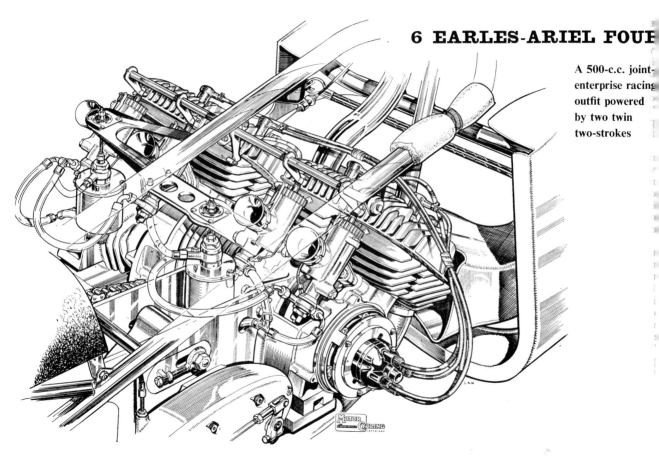

6 EARLES-ARIEL FOUR

A 500-c.c. joint-enterprise racing outfit powered by two twin two-strokes

YOU HAVE NEVER heard anything like it! And by 'it' I mean one of the most unusual British racers to be built for many a season—the Earles-Ariel sidecar outfit powered by a pair of modified 'Leader' engines coupled to form what is probably the first racing transverse-four two-stroke. . . .

Credit for the original concept of the machine must go to Ernie Earles, a man who is already assured of a niche in motorcycling history by his front fork design which has been adopted—and imitated by many manufacturers—almost literally throughout the world, especially on high-speedware.

It is one thing to have such an idea as this 'four', but something very different to put it into practice. Ernie emphasized that Ariel's, and particularly Clive Bennett, of their experimental shop, put in a terrific amount of work on the motor on the bench. But the outfit did not move under its own steam—or should I say scream?—until November 4, 1960. Then I was privileged to be amongst a party of journalists and members of the trade at the Mallory Park circuit, in

Detail of the finned cover joining the two 'Leader' engines and the large chassis tube.

Leicestershire, to see and hear that doyen of racing charioteers, Bill Boddice, put the new ensemble through its paces.

All heads craned as the outfit was wheeled from the van. We had been told the basic specification, but on the phone Ernie had been unduly modest about his part in the plan, for even the cycle parts show evidence of highly original thinking; the 'inside' arm of the chassis, for instance, is not attached to the nearside half of the cycle frame—it *is* the nearside half. From the offside the frame looks relatively orthodox, with swinging-fork rear suspension and a low riding position, but closer scrutiny reveals the thought and care that has

23

Offside, showing two of the large exhaust expansion chambers employed.

been put into it. The motor—or motors —is—or are—carried transversely, with the drive, from between the two units, taken to a Norton gearbox and clutch.

The engine itself, whilst highly original as racer, is almost production-line stuff! The port power-plant's crankcase has been machined to let the driving-shaft come out through the 'wrong' end and both motors have been given a fair amount of tuning—compression ratio is 12 : 1.

Carburation is by four Amal G.P. instruments with external needle-jet feed-pipes to prevent flooding because of the steep downdraught angle. Bore size is 1 in., main jet 220.

The engine coupling is unusual; each motor has an extra, outside, flywheel and from these the drive is taken by three pegs mounted in Silentbloc bushes, with a 7 : 1 safety factor.

Castor-base lubricant in 1 : 16 ratio is used and a faint haze is visible from the four exhaust pipe-expansion chamber terminals when the engine is running. The finned coil and batteries for the Lucas ignition equipment are stowed in the sidecar nose.

How did it go? I repeat—you've never heard anything like it! The power band is from about 6,000 to 8,500 r.p.m. with over 500 b.h.p. on tap. After a few 'warming-up' laps on his Norton, Bill set off on the four—which soon turned itself into a three when one plug went duff. Even so Bill, having to master a new machine, got the faulty Ariel to within three seconds of his Norton's time as a '375'. He came in for the plug fault to be remedied but, in the haste of the moment, a 'soft' plug had been put in the left inboard pot and the result was a burnt piston, stopping play for the day.

7 ROTARY-VALVE NORTON RACER

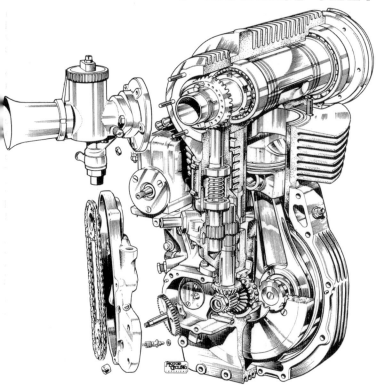

**An experimental power unit
developed in 1952-54**

A 500-c.c. 'MANX' Norton bottom
half with a rotary-valve cylinder head
grafted on to it—that, in a nutshell, is
the revolutionary racing motor which
Norton were developing in 1952–54.

It was at the 1951 Motorcycle Show
that designer Laurie Bond—the man
whose name is perpetuated by thousands of 'Minicars'—exhibited a rotary-
valve cylinder head, adapted for fitting
to a 500-c.c. Speedway J.A.P. engine,
on the B.A.C. stand. Race chief the late
Joe Craig of Norton liked the look of it
and Nortons took an option on the
motorcycle patent rights. They used an
86-mm. by 85·9-mm. 'Manx' motor to
take the head, Laurie Bond working on
the project at Norton's works.

On the J.A.P. the rotor had been
driven by chain, but to permit a 'Manx'
bottom end to be used it was adapted to
bevel drive. One can see the wisdom of
using a known lower engine assembly,

The rotary-valve head is deceptively simple to look at.

for all test results could be compared directly with the performance of a double-o.h.c. power plant of the poppet-valve type.

The rotary-valve head, as the illustrations show, lies 'across' the motor, so that the carburetter stands out on one side and the exhaust pipe on the other. It consists of a sleeved alloy casting in which the rotor is carried on two large-diameter bearings. A double-row ball unit gives positive end-location at the bevel-drive side; this avoids alterations in meshing due to expansion. Any 'growth' in length as temperature increases is allowed for by the employment of a heavy-duty parallel roller-race at the opposite side of the head.

As the head is wider than that of a 'Manx' unit, the vertical shaft of the bevel drive had to be stepped out to reach the end of the rotor. A virtue was made of this necessity by installing a gear-type oil pump at the 'step', so that the drive went in on one shaft of the pump and out on the other. The reason for the 'reversed' layout of the upper part of the drive, with the rotor bevels facing inwards, is simple; if the bevels had been assembled in the orthodox way, the rotor would have turned in the wrong direction for the port shapes, which had already been designed.

Oil is fed from the pump on the vertical shaft to the banjo casting that houses the bevels and it is then forced through the rotor, cooling it, and out via a union at the exhaust end. This coolant-cum-lubricant is entirely separate from the main engine oiling system; it is fed in at the base of the banjo and taken out from the top at the opposite end, so that complete flooding is always assured. Bleed holes at various points permit the excape of sufficient oil to lubricate the rotor itself. Longitudinal grooves retained the oil on the earlier rotors, but sealing blades, as used on the Wankel engine, were employed on the later-developed versions.

Gas sealing, always a problem with any type of valve, is critical with this pattern. Three annular grooves are cut in each end of the rotor, and rings are fitted in the outer and inner grooves of each group. Each centre groove lies

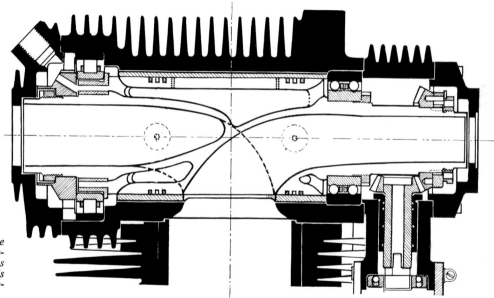

Cross-section of the complete head assembly. The rotor runs in a steel sleeve and is carried on two large-size bearings.

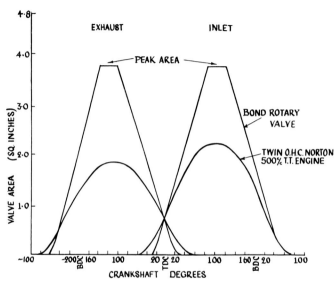

Graph showing the considerably greater increase in valve-opening area obtainable with the rotary valve compared with poppet valves for the same overlap. The flat top to the rotary-valve curve is accounted for by the valve port size being greater than the size of the combustion-chamber opening.
RIGHT: *Cross-section of the rotor showing the port shapes: note the lack of restriction.*

opposite to a drillway in the head casting, through which any 'pressure gas' that passes the inner ring can escape. The escape pipes can be seen on the front of the casting.

What are the advantages of this type of valve? It substitutes continuous motion in one direction for the reciprocating action of the poppet valve, which wastes energy because the inertia of the moving parts must be overcome every time their direction of motion is reversed (a handicap which desmodromic operation does not surmount). Further, for a given valve overlap, the rates of opening and closing can be very much faster with a rotary valve, and when the valve is fully open the rotary type will show a greatly increased free area for a given port size.

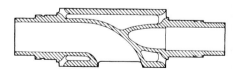

ROTARY-VALVE NORTON RACER

What are the snags? There is cost of machining; but this does not matter in a racing motor. Difficulties with sealing—a major problem with all types of rotary valve—gave their quota of trouble. Laurie Bond tells me that the Norton air-cooled motor experienced a lot of seizures due to uneven expansion of the head; at some points this caused sealing troubles, at other it created locally abnormal stresses which broke down the lubricant film. A similar engine was developed for the ill-fated Connaught G.P. car, but this was water-cooled and did not present such a great problem.

However, not all the troubles proved insurmountable and the power output was gradually increased from 35 b.h.p. to about 47 b.h.p.—roughly the same as the double-overhead-camshaft unit was producing at that time. Even when the power was there, and the seizures had been overcome, the team were not out of the wood, for it was frequently found that after the unit had been throttled down it could not be opened up again due to excessive oil in the combustion chamber.

It had been hoped to develop the unit sufficiently to enable it to be raced in the 1954 T.T., but Norton's policy changed and it was decided not to proceed with development.

Looking up into the head: the port edge shape of the rotor gives a slower cut off to the gas flow. Note waste pipes at the front.

A lubricant-retaining groove is machined between the ports.

8 ALF HAGON'S 350-c.c. KIRBY SPECIAL

Grass-track double-champion:
Alf Hagon's potent
J.A.P.-powered machine

THE NAME ALF HAGON will always be carved in the hall of fame of motor-cyclists, both as a speedway and grass-track rider and also as a builder of very good grass-track racers. These utilized a J.A.P. engine at first, although later he built models with B.S.A. 250-c.c. 'Star' units. All followed basically the same principle—light weight with good handling.

Alf's 350-c.c. Kirby Special, so-called after Romford dealer Tom Kirby, who supports him for grass events, broadly follows the general lines of many grass-track machines. Its power-plant is a four-stud J.A.P. unit, a smaller edition of the famous 500-c.c. speedway motor.

This is possibly the simplest racing motor built, a sturdy push-rod o.h.v. single, with wet-sump lubrication by means of a double Pilgrim pump which feeds the big-end and valve gear. It has a chain-driven B.T.H. magneto with fixed spark timing.

The cylinder head is of cast iron, but a Wellworthy 'Al-fin' barrel is fitted; both have the skimpiest of finning, thanks to the use of methanol, a much cooler-running fuel than petrol. Compression ratio is normally high and Alf uses a $1\frac{1}{16}$-in. bore T.T. carburetter, with remote float chamber, in place of the more usual track-type needle-less instrument.

Light-alloy plates of $\frac{5}{16}$ in. thickness, carrying an HTT Albion gearbox with 'semi-close' internals, join the motor to a decidedly spartan frame. (Alf builds his own frames, starting with a welding torch and a bundle of tubes!) The top and seat tubes act as an oil reservoir; Silentbloc bushes are used on the rear

---

IN BRIEF

Engine: Single-cylinder o.h.v.; 70-mm. bore × 90-mm. stroke = 344 c.c.; c.r. 13·5 : 1; no b.h.p. figures available.
Fuel tank: Steel $\frac{3}{4}$-gal. capacity.
Oil: 1 pt. carried in frame tubes.
Wheels: Steel rims carrying 2·75 in. × 21-in. Dunlop 'Trials Universal' at front, 3·50-in. × 19-in. modified Goodyear 'Grasshopper' at rear.
Weight: 245 lb.
Wheelbase: $56\frac{1}{2}$ in.

The subsidiary 'engine' plate which can be removed to allow the gearbox to be taken out of the frame and the pipe from the seat-pillar tube to the Pilgrim oil pump are unusual features.

The driving side reveals the remotely mounted float chamber and the hollow main frame bolts. Two small pipes from the rocket box lubricate the valve guides.

fork pivot and the suspension is controlled by Girling units. The front forks are standard undamped Metal Profiles components.

The rear hub is based on a 'rigid-type' B.S.A. component, with home-brewed K.O. spindle and light-alloy brake backplate. The seating, too, is 'A.H. special'.

Alf says that the front tyre seems to last for ever. The rear lasts a season, starting life as a Goodyear 'Grasshopper' and ending as an 'A.H.' for he laboriously cuts the tread to suit his own ideas. That they are the right ideas is evidenced by results!

YEARS AND YEARS ago Zeniths built a belt-drive machine which was so successful in competitions that it was barred from competing; half a century later four-cylinder 'fire-engines' built by the Meccanica Verghera Agusta factory at Gallarate, Italy, enjoyed almost as great a success in the 350- and 500-c.c. racing classes!

Although the four-cylinder M.V. is a fairly complex design it cannot by any means be called a freak, for it has proved itself to be one of the most reliable racing machines in use, needing less maintaining than the '125s' and '250s' that M.V.s ran. In John Surtees' experience, they were more reliable than production racers when driven fully extended.

I was surprised to learn that all the four-cylinder engines were built in 1951–52 and that very few or no modifications have been made to them. Most of the development was carried out on the frame and cycle parts, which have been tried, modified and re-tried.

Two types of front fork were available for riders, one had the spindle on the centre-line, the other had its spindle

carried on lugs forward of the stanchions. John Surtees preferred the former type, John Hartle the latter!

Main interest undoubtedly centres around the engine unit, which has a five-speed gearbox all included in the main castings. A pressed-up crankshaft is employed and complete discs rather than bob weights are used in each of the four 'little engines'. Crankshaft life is two years on the '500's and three years on the '350s'.

Steel connecting-rods with roller big-end bearings are used: the big-end has $\frac{3}{16}$-in. by $\frac{1}{4}$-in. rollers carried in Duralumin cages. On some models white-metal small-ends are used; on others the gudgeon pins run direct in the connecting-rods.

The engine has six main bearings—a roller bearing at each end and plain ones in between the crank compartments. Pistons each carrying three compression rings and with solid skirts are used and the cylinder-head shape approximates to a slightly flattened hemisphere. Drive to the twin overhead camshafts is by gears from the crankshaft through

a tunnel between the centre pair of cylinders. These two small gears take the drive to a large idler wheel which connects directly with gears formed on the centre of each camshaft. Valve angle is approximately 90°, although illustrations give the impression that this dimension is greater. John said this is because the cambox is slightly offset in relation to the centre line of the valves. The valves are operated through short tappets and each valve is returned by double coil springs. All four combustion chambers are in a single casting, but four separate cylinder barrels are employed.

Exhaust pipes are of approximately $1\frac{1}{2}$-in. diameter and each 'pot' has a separate pipe and megaphone. These megaphones have a slightly reversed cone-end, but this is probably for added strength rather than for any gain in power. The original, straight, megaphone tended to split at the ends, but the reverse ring welded on each gives strength at this vital point.

Carburation is by four Dell'Orto instruments, each pair having a flat float chamber situated longitudinally

John Surtees's 1959 Junior T.T.-winning machine.

IN BRIEF

Engine: Transverse four-cylinder, double o.h.c.; Junior 47-mm. bore × 49-mm. stroke = 350 c.c.; Senior, 52-mm. bore × 58-mm. stroke = 500 c.c.; c.r. 11·5: 1 on both engines; 43 b.h.p. at 10,200 r.p.m. for 350-c.c. engine and 56 b.h.p. at 9,800 r.p.m. for 500-c.c. unit.

Fuel tank: Light alloy, 8½-gal. capacity.

Oil: Carried in sump, approximately ¾ gal.

Wheels: Light-alloy rims carrying racing tyres, 3·00 in. × 19 in. front and 3·50 in. × 19 in. rear.

The four 'pots' are sparked by a horizontally mounted Lucas magneto.

bore size on the 350-c.c. engine is 23 mm. and that on the '500', 26 mm.

Ignition is provided by a Lucas racing four-cylinder magneto sparking through Lodge 10-mm. plugs; the instrument is driven by bevels off an auxiliary shaft running across the top of the gearbox and powered from the clutch gear. The gearbox breather is taken from this point and two pipes are led up to the outside edges of the inlet cambox.

Primary drive is by gears; one pinion on the engine shaft engages with the clutch gear and both have straight-cut teeth, as indeed do the gears used on the camshaft driving train. Internal ratios are not too close, except on fourth and top, as the engine has quite a flexible power output band; the internal ratios are often altered for use at different courses. Three solid Ferodo plates are used in the clutch and pressure is provided by five conventional coil springs. Gearchange, incidentally, is of the 'up-for-down' variety. Three litres of oil are carried in the sump.

The cycle parts of the machine are relatively conventional. The forks, apart

between them. The carburetter intakes, in plan view, taper in towards the rear of the machine and the induction pipes, too, are directed in towards the centre-line as they leave the head castings. This is to ensure that the rider has sufficient clearance by his knees, but it is possible, although I could get no confirmation, that a certain amount of swirl is imparted to the ingoing charge. Carburetter

The 3.50 by 19 in. rear tyre is Dunlop racing pattern.

Gearbox details are strictly orthodox: note the gearchange linkage and the exposed clutch-operating mechanism.

37

The twin front brakes are operated by a continuous cable running round a pulley adjoining the lever.

from the slight variation in trail provided by the different lower sliders, are fairly orthodox with coil springs and single-way hydraulic damping. The frame itself is of all-welded construction, using a variety of tubing shapes and fork members. The upper frame member changes its section from circular,

just under the seat, to oblong above the engine and then almost to square just behind the cylinder head. It is bolted into place, presumably to facilitate engine changing without dismantling, and at each end a U-tube is welded to it; the ends of each of these tubes, too, are bolted to the rest of the frame. The duplex down-members run from the steering-head right underneath the engine and sweep up to the seat position; fabricated brackets extend rearward to provide top anchorage in the suspension units. The pivoting fork operates on a bronze bush and, an unusual point, all sorts of suspension units are used, Woodhead-Munro, Girling or Armstrong, according to the rider's preference and the course on which the machines are being raced.

The front wheel has twin 10-in.-diameter, single-leading-shoe brakes and the shoes themselves are relatively narrow—about $\frac{3}{4}$-in. across. Large air scoops are provided and the front brake lever has a remarkable compensating and adjusting device so that the rider can take up wear during the race with-

out affecting the individual brake settings. The back brake shoe is $1\frac{1}{4}$ in. wide, but again the single-leading-shoe type is used. The rear sprocket is remote from the hub and rubber grommets around the fixing-bolts provide a degree of cushioned drive.

The chain-oiler oil-tank is included in the rear of the racing seat for the T.T., but is not used for other races. For this event an $8\frac{1}{2}$-gal. fuel tank is mounted; fuel consumption is the same on both the 350- and 500-c.c. machines. The $8\frac{1}{2}$ gallons is sufficient for four laps with a substantial reserve. Elementary mathematics show that the machines do about 18 m.p.g., which is not bad, considering the speed they pack!

The 'In brief' details provide some of the answers to power output and the figures given are for b.h.p. at the rear wheel and not at the engine shaft. The maximum revs. can be exceeded by about 300 r.p.m. on each engine with safety, although this is not normally done, as the power then falls off slightly. The rev-counters fitted to the machines register up to 12,000 r.p.m.

A liquid-cooled double o.h.c. '500' and the 125-c.c. single used for bench tests

The Norton that never was! As visualized by a 'Motor Cycling' artist.

BACK IN THE early fifties, rumour on many occasions (and the late Joe Craig on one) had spoken of a Norton four-cylinder racer. When the project was finally shelved, no word appeared in print—and the general public were led to believe that rumour had again been wrong. But it hadn't!

There was a 'four'—designed by the team responsible for the original B.R.M. racing car. Norton's still had some parts of the engine in 1959. They also had a complete single-cylinder 125-c.c. unit which was used for prolonged bench testing—this engine being literally a quarter of the four from the crankcase upwards.

The 'four' was a compact, liquid-cooled, engine, mounted transversely with the cylinders slightly inclined. The gearbox was built in unit.

In 1959 only the crankcase and head castings and the crankshaft remained. The photographs show these historic relics. When I viewed them at Brace-bridge Street, race-shop chief Doug Hele told me that all work on the four had been abandoned long before he had taken over, and little in the way of information was on record.

A machined and finished head, complete, had been lying in the works some months before, but this could no longer be found; however, the casting gives some idea of what the finished job would have been like. We were in luck with the bottom half of the engine, for a machined crankcase—complete with five-bearing

TOP: *One of the wet, screw-in lines with the Elektron sump and alloy crankcase castings.*

BELOW: *The crankcase and the housing for the gearbox shafts (engine inverted).*

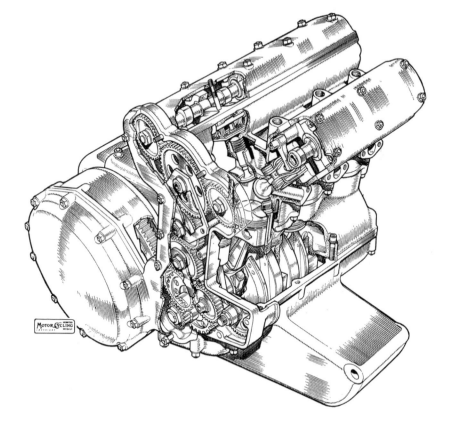

This drawing of the engine shows the arrangement of the timing-gear train and its steady plates. Magneto drive is taken from a forward extension. The cutaway cylinder liner reveals the screwed top section and double 'O' rings for sealing.

MOTOR CYCLING WEEKLY

crankshaft, was found; this showed the amount of care that went into the design—all the studs, for example, are waisted on their unthreaded portions.

The sectioned drawings shows the crankshaft layout. For each of the two inboard cylinders there is one full fly-wheel and one bobweight; outboard on each side are two bobweights. All big-end and main bearings are plain shell-type components. The primary drive is by a gear-wheel carried inboard of the timing-side outer main bearing.

The double overhead camshafts are driven by a Y-shaped train of gears carried in a large light-alloy oil bath. Steady plates are provided between the gear-wheel spindles so that no distortion shall take place at high r.p.m. A forward extension of the drive turns the special racing magneto.

Each wet cylinder liner is screwed into the head individually. When the head-and-liners assembly has been 'offered down' to the crankcase, the liners are sealed at their lower ends by rubber rings. As the unit was designed for liquid cooling there was no necessity

In this cross-section through the engine the disposition of internal flywheels and bobweights and primary drive gear can be examined. The sectioning of the two inner cylinders has been angled to pass through the inlet valve (left) and exhaust valve (right) with its finned, water-cooled guide.

for the exhaust ports to face forward, and they are, in fact, at the back. Four separate forward-facing carburetters are specified, although one imagines that they would not benefit from being supplied with warm air from the radiator immediately in front of them!

Special attention has been paid to cooling the exhaust-valve guides; they are finned and pressed into the head so that coolant can circulate around their midriffs. In the sectional drawing, the section has been 'bent' on the inner cylinders to give a line through the inlet valve (left) and exhaust valve (right), and it will be seen that double hairpin springs are used. A slipper-type cam follower is interposed between each valve and the camshaft.

Oil, carried in a large Elektron sump casting, is fed from a submerged gear pump to a gallery along the back of the cylinders and thence to the big-ends via the central main bearing.

No one is really certain whether the four ran—but the '125' definitely did. A guinea-pig for the four, it was the subject of steady development on the

RIGHT: *The 125-c.c. test engine crankshaft is exceptionally massive.*

BELOW: *In the centre of this photograph is the water pump used during bench tests.*

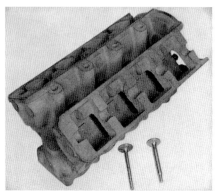

Top view of an unmachined cylinder-head casting, and a pair of valves. Note the difference in stem diameters: so designed that the exhaust valve head remains cool.

test-bench. It was not intended for use in a machine.

The single-cylinder unit is split horizontally in four places. The head bolts on to the barrel—a separate item in this motor—which is secured by four studs to the crankcase. The crankcase itself is split on the plane of the crankshaft, a bolted-on sump making the final layer of the sandwich.

The photographs show most of the details clearly. Unfortunately, the engine was only lightly assembled when photographing started—the timing case, for some obscure reason, would not go home properly. Only later did we find that someone had put the crankshaft in its housing the wrong way round!

The single ran on a 9 : 1 compression ratio and had valves with head diameters of $1\frac{3}{16}$ in. for the inlet and $1\frac{3}{32}$ in. for the exhaust. The valves were at 30° to the vertical instead of the more usual 45°.

The engine was running on the bench in November, 1953, but the development was concentrated initially upon performance at relatively low r.p.m. The design showed some promise, but at this stage policy dictated that production machines should have first claim upon research and Norton's never completed the four.

11 REG DEARDEN'S SUPERCHARGED VINCENT

1000 c.c. o.h.v.
vee-twin power
unit for 'world's
fastest' machine

The S.U. carburetter is of 2¾-in. bore and was made especially for this engine. An oil reservoir for the supercharger lies just below the foot-change linkage rod.

THE VINCENT WAS built to the special order of Reg Dearden by the Stevenage concern in 1950 and Reg estimates it had cost him about £5,000. Work on his fleet of road-racers pushed the Vincent into the background for a time, but in 1957 it was stripped and the bottom-end rebuilt with much-larger-than-normal main bearings and a prototype 'Picador' big-end.

Since then the heads have been much altered and new valves fitted—Nimonic inlet and sodium-cooled exhaust. The machine is, at first glance, very similar to a standard 'Black Lightning', with Girdraulic front forks and pivoting rear suspension; actually, very little of it is standard.

The engine is a 50° twin with the same bore and stroke measurements, 84 mm. × 90 mm., as all post-war production Vincents, but most of the moving parts are 'one-offs'. Reg was, naturally

enough, somewhat reticent about details of the power unit. The bottom end is almost entirely on the secret list. The most significant disclosable fact about the upper works is that special Wellworthy pistons give a compression ratio of 12 : 1.

The Lucas racing magneto is also 'one-off'—a description that seemed to recur every time Reg mentioned any part of the machine.

Centre of attractions is undoubtedly the Shorrocks vane-type supercharger. It is 9 in. in diameter and is driven by an extra chain from the gearbox clutch to

---

IN BRIEF

Engine: 50° Vee-twin o.h.v.; 84-mm. bore × 90-mm. stroke = 998 c.c.; c.r. 12 : 1; 130 b.h.p. at 6,800 r.p.m.

Ignition: Lucas racing magneto.

Carburation: 2¾-in. bore S.U. instrument feeding via 9-in. Shorrocks vane-type supercharger.

Wheels: Steel rims with Avon record-type tyres. 3·00 in. × 21 in. front, 3·50 in. × 20 in. rear.

Wheelbase: 64 in.

a second clutch on the blower shaft. Alterations of sprocket size can be used to vary the 'blow' from 8 lb. per sq. in. to some 20 lb. per sq. in.

Also unique, the S.U. carburetter has a bore size of 2½ in.—almost room to walk in and clean the jets. The massive float chamber has a balsa-wood float.

The engine produces about 130 b.h.p. at 6,800 r.p.m., a rev. limit which has been set to reduce the chances of a blow-up. There is a separate oil tank and feed to the blower; this can be seen just below the gearchange link rod.

To acommodate the chain drive to the blower, the gearbox has been built up with an extra-long mainshaft and the drive-side crankcase has been altered. The primary and blower transmissions are all carried inside one very 'arge casing.

The machine has Girdraulic forks with sidecar-strength springs and a longer frame-backbone member. The rear sub-frame has been lengthened to permit more tyre growth at speed, and made stronger to cope with the great power increase over the standard 'Black

Broadside view of the machine accentuates its long wheelbase. The tyres fitted are not the type that would be used in a record attempt.

Lightning'. Extra-heavy rear suspension springs are employed to cope with the extra weight—Reg could not quote a weighbridge figure for the complete machine, but it is safe to say that it is around 500 lb.!

The wheels and tyres at present fitted are not those that will be used for record attempts—special rims and covers have to be employed for these—but are merely 'jury-rigs' on which the machine can be wheeled around in the shop.

Reg Dearden hoped to take the machine to Utah for the record attempt during 1960, but plans went wrong; he later sold the machine.

The 1959 'double-knocker' Honda twin, '125'

TO SEND FIVE riders, a group of mechanics, five racing machines, four practice mounts and enough spares and tools to set up a completely self-contained workshop and depot to the Isle of Man is expensive, even if the *équipe* comes only from the mainland. To send them from Japan, the personnel by air, probably costs more than many factories spend on racing development in a twelve month.

Yet that is what the Japanese Honda factory did in 1959. It gives some indication of the confidence they have in their machines—and, incidentally, shakes the lately popular fallacy that the Isle of Man races are losing their stature.

Another popular fallacy is that the Japanese are copyists. There might have been some evidence for this in their very early post-war models, but the Honda racer is, without any doubt at all, basically original.

A parallel twin of 'over-square' dimensions, the engine/gear unit has a vertical shaft drive to the front overhead camshaft. Light alloy is used for all main castings, including the cylinder head, which are integral with each other. A K.L.G. 10-mm. plug, centrally located in each combustion chamber, is sparked

A scoop to force air between the cam-box and the tops of the head fins is mounted on the rear of the cambox.

IN BRIEF

Engine: Parallel twin, double o.h.c.; 41-mm. bore × 41-mm. stroke = 124·7 c.c.; no c.r. figure available; approx. 18·5 b.h.p. at 14,000 r.p.m.
Fuel tank: Light-alloy, 3½-gal. capacity.
Oil: Carried in sump, approx. ½ gal.
Wheels: Light-alloy rims carrying Avon racing tyres 2·50 in. × 19 in. front, 2·75 in. × 18 in. rear.
Weight: 176 lb.

by a magneto mounted at the end of the inlet camshaft.

Primary transmission is by gear to the clutch, which is carried on the mainshaft of the six-speed gearbox, whence final drive is by chain.

The engine's output is claimed to be 18·5 b.h.p. at 14,000 r.p.m. That is 148 b.h.p. per litre, which should give the opposition something to think about!

External pipes indicate that oil is fed to the cylinder walls—or it could be routed through drillways on the cylinder castings to the camgear, though this seems unlikely, as other pipes go there anyway. A heavily ribbed sump under the crankcase, similar to that used in the A.J.S. 'Porcupine' twins, carries 2 litres of oil. The crankcase itself is also deeply finned and split horizontally.

Carburation is by twin Keihin instruments of unspecified bore, and the exhausts have exceptionally long, tapered megaphones with very slight reverse coning. Gear-changes and brake pedals are on the opposite sides to normal British practice, the gear lever having heel-and-toe operation.

The cycle parts are fairly straightforward—leading-link front forks (the links being connected by a loop, like those of the Greeves), a 'tubular-spine' frame and pivoting-fork rear suspension. Fore and aft, suspension is controlled by coil springs with hydraulic damping, and the rear units are made in the Honda factory. The layout of the front suspension is very similar to that of the production machine.

Massive light-alloy hubs conceal 180-mm.-diameter brakes, that at the rear of single-leading-shoe pattern. The rear wheel sprocket is remote from the hub, being bolted to it at points near its centre. Rims are of light alloy and Avon racing tyres are used. The front rim at 19 in. is 1 in. larger in diameter than the rear. This could be to give greater ground clearance, or to improve handling characteristics.

The rev.-counter, is carried on the head extension tube, and the fact that it is calibrated to 14,000 r.p.m. would suggest that the race engines are developing peak power around the 12,500–13,000 r.p.m. band.

Close-up of the power unit shows clearly the vertical camshaft drive, the heavily finned sump and crankcase, and the oil leads to the cylinder walls.

13 GREENWOOD-TRIUMPH COMBINATION

**The first British outfit to finish
in the 1959 Sidecar T.T.**

Add holes—add lightness.

IN BRIEF

Engine: Parallel-twin o.h.v.; either 63-mm. bore × 80-mm. stroke = 498 c.c. (9·5 : 1 c.r.); or 71-mm. bore × 82-mm. stroke = 649 c.c. (8·5 : 1 c.r.); no b.h.p. figures available; peak r.p.m. 7,600–7,800 on 500 c.c., 7,500 on 650 c.c.

Fuel tank: Glass fibre, 2½- or 6-gal. capacity according to circuit.

Oil tank: Glass fibre, 13-pt. capacity, 1 gal. in use.

Wheels: Light-alloy rims carrying Dunlop racing tyres, 3·00 in. × 18 in. front, 4·00 in. × 16 in. rear, 3·50 in. × 12 in. sidecar.

Weight: 650 c.c., 350 lb.; 500 c.c., 340 lb.

BY FAR THE most exciting duel for a place in the entire 1959 T.T. series was that fought out for sixth berth in the sidecar race between Owen Greenwood on his Triumph-powered 'special' and L. Neussner on a B.M.W.

At the end of the ninth lap Greenwood had let Neussner go by in the mistaken belief that this was Schneider, the race leader, lapping him! He fought to overcome his disadvantage in a wheel-to-wheel battle throughout the ultimate lap, but did not succeed in getting past the German until Bedstead Corner—a left-hander where the B.M.W., with its right-hand chair, was at a theoretical advantage—less than a mile from the finish. At Governor's, Greenwood had a short lead, but the superior power of the B.M.W. enabled it to catch the Triumph, the outfits finishing almost abreast with the German some 15 m.p.h. faster—but on the line, where it mattered, The Triumph still had a few inches advantage.

What is this 'special' that managed to head all Nortons and several B.M.W.s? There is nothing revolutionary about it—just sound engineering and carefully applied common sense.

Two engines are available. For Grands Prix, where the capacity limit is 500 c.c., a 498-c.c. Triumph 'Tiger 100' twin is fitted; for other events a 649-c.c. 'Tiger 110' unit is employed. The latter was installed when I saw the outfit, and is shown in the illustrations. The main external difference between the two is that a standard cast-iron barrel is used on the '650', whereas the '500' has its standard die-cast alloy muff with steel liners.

The inlet valves have been trimmed to give slightly narrower-than-standard seating surface so that they do not obstruct the incoming charge. Big-ends are plain Vandervell shell bearings, whilst ball thrust bearings are employed for driving and timing side mains. Ignition is by Lucas racing magneto and carburation by twin Amal GP10 instruments, with bore sizes of $1\frac{3}{32}$ in. and $1\frac{3}{16}$ in. on the small and big engines respectively. Castor-base oil is used and 100-octane fuel.

The fuel supply system is interesting.

A pump mounted on the timing chest raises petrol from the tank in the nose of the sidecar to a home-brewed weir-type float chamber. Externally this is a normal-looking component with a feed into the top. The fuel passes down an internal tube, which almost touches the base of the chamber and then overflows, after filling a larger-diameter tube attached to the base of the float chamber, to an outer section whence it drains back to the tank.

Transmission is via a Triumph close-ratio gearbox and a standard clutch with Ferodo inserts. The fact that Owen saves 2¼ lb. from the internals of the gearbox without altering any critical parts is indicative of the care he puts into his machine.

The main frame was designed, and the tubes bent up by Ernie Walker and subsequently brazed by Owen himself. The swinging fork is another Walker component; it pivots on Silentbloc bushes.

Front forks are cut-down 'Manx' Norton and the wheel hubs are of similar origin. One advantage of the frame design is that the Triumph motor can be lifted straight out through the top tubes, after undoing the reamer-fitted engine bolts and the ancillary fittings.

The sidecar chassis was made by Don Houghton to his and Owen's design. It is exceedingly light and is attached to the bike by the simplest of connections. Small ears brazed to sidecar and machine tubes are joined by telescopic struts with strengthened, flattened ends—another weight-saving plan.

Three-millimetre plywood, suitably strutted, is used for floor covering—lightness again—but the main weight-saving device is the liberal use of glass fibre in the outfit. Sidecar body, sidecar mudguard, engine cowl, oil tank, fuel tank, seat-cum-tail-section and frontal fairing are all of this material. The fairing, complete with rev-counter and fittings, weighs only 15 lb! Total weight of the complete outfit is almost 100 lb. lighter than an equivalent roadster solo.

Bird's-eye view of the engine shows how the frame tubes have been splayed to give adequate clearance.

J. Terry's 250-c.c.
sprint 'special'

AT THE RAMSGATE sprint in October 1958 John Terry and his 249-c.c. Ariel won their class—which was not entirely unexpected by the *cognoscenti*, for this combination of man and machine had done precisely the same thing at the previous fifteen sprints entered, and that covered almost every event of the kind since 1955. A bent valve at the Cheltenham meeting in 1955, caused by 'someone' blipping the throttle too hard in the paddock, made a break in winning sequence, but since then the record had been monotonous. Times generally have been about 15·2 seconds for the

---

IN BRIEF

Engine: Single-cylinder o.h.v.; 61-mm. bore × 84-mm. stroke = 249 c.c.; c.r. 10 : 1; no b.h.p. figure available; peak r.p.m., 7,400.
Fuel tank: Light alloy, 2-gal. capacity.
Oil tank: Light alloy, 4-pt. capacity.
Wheels: Light-alloy rims carrying Dunlop tyres. 2·75 in. × 19 in. front, 3·25 in. × 18 in. rear.
Wheelbase: 53 in.
Weight: 230 lb.

standing quarter-mile and 31 seconds for the standing kilometre.

John is a member of the motorcycle trade: his business makes pannier equipment of all types and sizes, and the Ariel is essentially a spare-time occupation. He purchased it in 1945, in almost new condition. It was a 1939 trials model, and at first John used it for trials and scrambles. However, the lure of speed made itself felt and eventually his interest was focused on sprint work to the exclusion of cross-country events.

Since that change of policy, the model has been steadily developed by its owner and his business associate, Len Collins, the latter doing most of the work to the power plant. The results have been, to say the least, encouraging, and the machine's performance is such that it occasionally gains a place in the 350-c.c. class at quarter-mile sprints.

The power unit has been modified in many details by its tuners. A Royal Enfield light-alloy connecting-rod, modified to take the Ariel uncaged roller big-end, is now fitted; there is no small-end bush, the gudgeon pin running direct on

An excellent impression of the size of the finning on the home-built cylinder barrel is gained in this view of the engine's timing side.

the alloy. Main bearings are of standard size, but lipped rollers have been substituted for the ball-bearings originally specified. Hepolite supplied the piston, but a light-alloy barrel was made up to the tuners' own design from DTD424 metal, with a cast-iron liner. The finning was deliberately made extra large to dissipate as much heat as possible, as the original cast-iron head is still employed. The head has been metal-sprayed with the aluminium powder, but whether this is beneficial is debatable.

The internals of the timing-chest have been drastically revised. Special cams with vernier adjustment have been made up and the original oil pump has been discarded in favour of a Triumph component; lubrication is by a very light-grade mineral oil. Carburation is by $1\frac{1}{16}$-in. bore Amal TT9 instrument and 100-octane fuel is generally used.

Light-alloy engine plates have been built up. They extend rearwards to carry the Triumph gearbox, which has had the kick-starter cut off and a G.P.-type clutch fitted.

The rigid frame has been strengthened at the rear. At one time John modified the frame to take rear springing, but this proved faulty; weight, in any case, was supremely important, so he reverted to a rigid rear end. Front suspension has been improved by the adoption of A.M.C. 'Teledraulic' forks and wheel. The forks have a home-built crown lug and clip-on bars.

That there is nothing freakish about the machine is apparent from the illustrations. It shows just what can be done with relatively small resources and patient work.

Power unit detail showing the shock-absorberless engine-shaft sprocket.

The most successful privately built
road racer of 1959

NOT SO LONG ago the chances of Britain having a machine on the leader-board in a 250-c.c. international race were negligible. Italy and Germany held sway, and of the few British models on the grid most were built around pre-war power plants by Rudge, Excelsior and Velocette—very good motors in their day, but obviously not comparable with modern products of factory development.

No British factory has shown any interest in the racing quarter-litre since Velocette withdrew a decade ago. This indifference, however, has served as a spur to 'privateers'. Two of the most promising of these entered for the 250-c.c. Lightweight T.T. of 1959. Bob Geeson's R.E.G. twin, unhappily, fell out when in the running for leader-board placing; but Tommy Robb, brilliant up-and-coming Ulsterman, achieved a resounding success by bringing the G.M.S. (Geoff. Monty Special) home in fourth berth, beaten only by the M.V.s of Provini, Ubbiali and Chadwick. A success which he repeated in the Ulster G.P.

The G.M.S. story started in the winter of 1955–56, when Geoff, already well known as a 'privateer', built two identical frames, one of which now equips the successful '250'.

Mild-steel 2¼-in.-diameter tubing of 16 g.-wall thickness is used for the main backbone member and the front down-tubes are 1¼ in. 18 g. T45-grade steel. The swinging fork is welded-up from

The large-diameter front down-tubes of the 'open' frame mate with the front engine plates. The nearside tube is a reservoir for the primary chain oiler.

The front forks are Norton 'Roadholder'. The twin-leading-shoe brake is to be converted to 'all-cable' operation.

16 g. pressings—a practice independently followed by Ariels, incidentally, although G.M. has used it since the later 1940s. Dural plate, $\frac{5}{16}$-in. thick, is used for the rear sub-frame side members, and the engine-gearbox plates.

Girling units control the rear suspension with modified Norton 'Roadholder' forks at the front. The head angle is the same as that of the 'Featherbed' Norton, but the wheelbase, at 52 in., is slightly shorter.

Both wheels are Norton. The front hub has been carved out to save weight. The frame is unconventional in that it is of 'open' pattern, but Geoff points out that it was designed to take an engine-gearbox assembly that would be ultra-stiff and yet quickly detachable.

The oil tank, which has more corners and angles than any other I have seen, is of light alloy and snuggles in the space bounded by the engine, the gearbox and their connecting-plates. One would expect the oil to get extraordinarily hot, but in practice its running temperature is only 140–145°F., and although the frames's offside down-tube is plugged and tapped for use as an oil cooler, it has not been found necessary to bring it into circuit. (The nearside tube forms a reservoir for the chain oiler.) A black surface on the engine and oil tank definitely helps to keep the temperature down. The gearbox is an ordinary Norton 'Manx' unit, quite unmodified.

So to the engine. 'B.S.A. cut down' is often airily used to describe the G.M.S. unit, but a second glance will show that, whilst Small Heath supplied the original castings for the major components, someone else has done a lot of original work in this department.

IN BRIEF

Engine: Single-cylinder o.h.v.; 72-mm. bore × 61-mm. stroke = 247 c.c.; c.r. 8·3 : 1; no b.h.p. figures available; engine peaks at 8,200–8,400 r.p.m.

Fuel tank Light alloy, 4¼-gal. capacity.

Oil tank: Light alloy, 6 pt. capacity.

Wheels: Light-alloy rims carrying Avon racing tyres, 3·00 in. × 19 in. front, 3·25 in. × 19 in. rear.

Weight: 250 lb.

Wheelbase: 52 in.

The head casting has an induction port in the same plane as the centre-line of the machine; this has been achieved by boring through into the combustion space and welding a large-bore tube in place.

Downdraught angle is the same as on the '350' B.S.A. Length of the parallel-bore induction tract is about 11-in.— not quite so long as it at first appears. Valves are modified '350 Gold Star'. Sparks come from the centrally located 10-mm. K.L.G. plug of TE280 rating.

A 'rebore-size' B.S.A. '350' piston is carried on a steel connecting-rod which has a split big-end eye with a Vandervell lead-bronze shell bearing. The small-end is a standard bronze bush. Oil pressure (using a castor-base lubricant) is 25 lb. per sq. in. to the big-end. The barrel liner, of close-grained cast iron, has a B.S.A. muff over it; a four-'thou.' interference fit permits the hot-and-cold assembly method to be used without pressing.

The one-piece crankshaft is a complete break-away from normal 'Gold Star' practice. Geoff has made it from a high-quality steel and has included integral bobweights. It runs on a roller-bearing on the timing side and ball-and-roller components on the driving side. The flywheel is outside and 9-in. diameter; though apparently $\frac{3}{4}$-in. thick, it is actually hollowed out to give an overall thickness of $\frac{1}{4}$ in. on 'lip' and body.

Timing gear is as 'Gold Star', except for the use of hollow RR56 light-alloy forged tappets instead of solid-steel components. Valve and ignition timing (42° advance) are standard.

The model's 'long' look is the result of its small overall height. A couple or so inches lower and 100 c.c. smaller than a 350 'Manx', it pulls, course for course, the same overall gear, except for an inch difference in the rear-wheel diameter.

The carburetter, with its $1\frac{9}{32}$-in. choke, looks big and is big. I was surprised to learn that Geoff has many times confirmed that the same carburetter size, induction-pipe length and jet size can prove right for 250-, 350- and 500-c.c. motors! On the exhaust system the same applies. The pipe length and shape on the G.M.S. give ample power at low r.p.m. for slow corners.

16 THE BEETON-HARRIS B.M.W. OUTFITS

**German engines, Reynolds frames
and Watsonian sidecars
make potent racers**

TWO OF BRITAIN'S top-line chariot-
ers, 'Pip' Harris and Jack Beeton, made
news in 1959 when running a B.M.W.
outfit with great success. 'Pip' drove it
most of the time, but it was, in fact, a
joint-ownership venture. For the 1960
season they built a couple of B.M.W.
'specials' based on the knowledge gained
in the fun and games of 1959.

The machines are identical apart from
brakes and streamlining, but the sidecars, although both Watsonian, do have
differences.

The power unit is one of the well-
known B.M.W. 'Rennsport', engines
with integral five-speed gearbox and
shaft drive. Each cylinder has a single
overhead camshaft driven by shaft and
bevel gears; the drive shaft has a splined
coupling which enables quick changes of
compression ratio to be made without

Carburetter details of Beeton's machine, which has a different design of swill pots to Harris's model.

any need for odd spacers and packing pieces.

The cylinder heads are of light alloy, with sodium-cooled exhaust valves, but the barrels are cast iron.

The Munich works gave the engine a thorough overhaul during the winter and Jack says they are reluctant to tell him much about what goes inside! Still, we do know that it has needle roller-bearing big-ends with roller drive-side and ball timing-side mains. Ignition is by Bosch rotating-magnet magneto.

On any racing B.M.W. engine the induction side is worth studying—I doubt if many are identical—and the J.B. motor is no exception. Dell'Orto carburetters of 32-mm. bore are fed by Amal float chambers; to make these look even more impressive, Jack has his own design of 'swill-pot' carried inboard of each mixing chamber to balance the fuel under the forces involved in brisk cornering.

On the B.M.W. the final drive shaft is carried inside the swinging fork. Jack tells me that the frame has been built so that if need be, the motor can be

shifted forward to put more weight on the front wheel; but if this has to be done it will be necessary to fix an outrigger bearing and a short intermediate shaft, because the angularity of the swinging fork at full travel gives only just enough clearance on the drive shaft at present.

The frame has been specially made by the Reynolds Tube Co. Ltd. from '531' tubing. Of all-brazed construction, it is both lighter and lower than the B.M.W. type. In principle it is similar to the usual run of duplex frames which are variations on the Norton 'Featherbed' theme. An extra bracing tube from the steering-head top runs to a cross-tube above the motor.

Pick-up points for the full streamlining are brazed on, as are the cross-tubes for carrying the sidecar connection ears. The forks are of Reynold-Earles pattern, with brazed-up head and crown lugs.

Suspension all round is controlled by Girling units; the wheels are B.M.W. with cable-and-rod-operated brakes.

The sidecar is based on 'Pip's' 1959 model, with much rehashing by Watsonian's Ben Willits. It has a 12-in. wheel. Both the guard and the sidecar nose are glass-fibre material, but the machine streamlining is of light alloy.

'Pip's outfit differs in that the sidecar is of improved design, with dished floor and alloy guard and nose-piece. His streamlining has a more upswept nose and is lighter than Jack's, and hydraulic brakes are fitted all round.

IN BRIEF

Engine : B.M.W. o.h.c. horizontally opposed twin; 66-mm. bore × 72-mm. stroke = 492 c.c.; c.r. 9·75 : 1; no performance figures available.
Fuel: 6-gal. light-alloy tank.
Oil: 6-pt. carried in sump.
Wheels: Light-alloy rims carrying Dunlop racing tyres, 3·50 in. × 16 in. front and rear, 3·50 in. × 12 in. sidecar.
Wheelbase: 56¼ in.

Rear end of the Beeton machine.

The most successful sprinter of 1960

DURING 1960 THE combination of Charlie Luck and his Norton Special were almost unbeatable in sprints. Their best times over a standing quarter-mile during the summer were 12·66 seconds at Blackpool and 12·64 seconds at Ramsgate.

Charlie points out that a lot of the credit for its success must go to his near-neighbour in Worcestershire Bill Stuart, who has done a vast amount of work on the engine and has generally directed proceedings.

IN BRIEF

Engine: Norton d.o.h.c.; 86-mm. bore × 86-mm. stroke = 499 c.c.; 10·75 : 1 c.r.; approximately 52 b.h.p. at 7,400 r.p.m.

Transmission: Norton four-speed racing-type gearbox internals.

Fuel: 1-pt. steel tank.

Oil: 6-pt. steel tank.

Wheels: Light-alloy rims carrying 2·75 in. × 21 in. front tyre and Dunlop 'Sidecar Racing' 3·50 in. × 19 in. rear tyre.

Weight: 245 lb.

The engine in the Special is basically a long-stroke racer on to which a short-stroke flywheel assembly, barrel and pistons have been grafted. Actually, the motor is built up from a lot of odd parts; for instance, the crankcase halves did not belong to each other.

Both main bearings have steel housings retained in the crankcase halves by Allen screws. The drive side has a couple of roller-bearings, whereas on the timing side one roller-bearing and one ball-bearing are used. An Alpha big-end assembly is fitted and the piston is a standard short-stroke type machined with a wider squish land to fit the original long-stroke head.

Originally, a very special piston was used which had been made from a blank by Charlie. This had been lightened very extensively. Unfortunately, this piston showed signs of cracking when inspected half-way through the season and it was changed.

The cylinder head has a wider valve angle than is used on a short-stroke. The valves themselves are slightly smaller than on the current motors. KE805 is

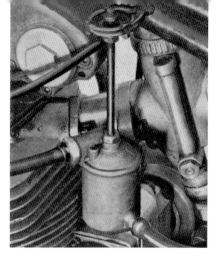

The $1\frac{17}{32}$ in. G.P. carburetter uses a S.U. float chamber.

the material of the slightly tulip-shaped inlet valve, while the flat-headed exhaust valve is made of KE965.

The cylinder head is of light alloy with cast-iron inlet and bronze exhaust inserts. The inlet port is not parallel, but is tapered towards the valve head and the GP carburetter has been bored out an extra $\frac{1}{32}$-in. from its original $1\frac{1}{2}$-in. diameter. The remotely mounted float chamber came from S.U. carburetter.

Every effort has been made to reduce friction in the motor and the vertical bevel shaft now runs on a ball-journal

If the head-steady bolts and distance pieces are removed, head and cambox can be taken off normally.

and a steady bush at each end. The motor itself runs on petrol and is estimated to give about 52–53 b.h.p. Although maximum power is developed around 7,300 r.p.m., the engine will rev to 8,000 without bursting. For a kilometre event, the machine is geared to give 7,200 r.p.m. in top; this actually produces a speed of around 130 m.p.h. at the end of the kilometre from a standing start.

The motor is only half the story of this machine, for it is carried in a very nice duplex frame that, although it looks as if it had been made for the job, was originally intended for a 'Grand Prix' New Imperial of about 1936.

Ex-Velocette Webb girder forks are used, and a non-adjustable steering-damper is fitted underneath. This is kept fairly tight, as is the single side-damper—Charlie took off the other side-damper in his weight-saving campaign.

The origin of the oil tank is fairly obvious from the photograph. It has three internal baffle plates to stop frothing. Although the tank will hold about 4 pt., only $1\frac{1}{2}$ pt. are in circulation.

The fuel tank, of soldered tin, will hold 1 pt., but in fact only $\frac{1}{2}$ pt. is normally put in. Both tanks are mounted on sponge rubber.

The gearbox started life as ex-W.D.; the layshaft has been cut at the kick-starter end, and the end-cover blanked off. Cutting the shaft exposed its soft centre and this has been drilled $\frac{3}{8}$ in. for lightness for most of its length. The plain bearing at the K.S. end has been replaced by a ball journal. The internals are virtually 'Manx' except that the bottom gear is rather lower—Daytona gearing. The short frame does not allow enough room to take the later type of 'Manx' gearbox.

The drive reaches the road through a 'Sidecar Racing' rear tyre, chosen for its flat tread form, which gives more traction.

The persistent search for weight reduction has obviously paid dividends, and the little bits and pieces taken off here and there result in an all-up weight for rider and machine of just under 400 lb., which will give food for thought to some stouter sprinters!

66

Forerunner of a world champion

ONE OF THE highlights of the 1959 T.T. series was the appearance of the 125.-c.c. twin-cylinder Hondas. Japanese racing machines making their first visit to the Island. That they carried off the team prize is now history.

Later that year the Honda factory raced a 250-c.c. 'four' in Japan, the forerunner of a model that was to score such resounding successes during the following seasons.

Readers will recall that the 125.-c.c. racer has an inclined engine with the camshaft drive taken from the nearside;

the sump is split horizontally and separate carburetters and coils are used for each 'pot'. The newcomer is similar except that it has vertical cylinders and the camshaft drive on the opposite side of the unit. The cycle parts of the '250' are also very like the 125-c.c. twin, and obviously many engine parts are interchangeable, as bore and stroke dimensions are the same on both.

Five of these machines were entered in the Asama Locano circuit race in August 1959 and at that time the factory announced a brief specification for them (see 'In Brief'). The claimed power output was 35 b.h.p. at 14,000 r.p.m. As the Asama circuit is on rough roads the model shown has 'semi-knobbly' tyres, orthodox handlebars and no streamlining, but a completely new frame and model shown has 'semi-knobbly' tyres, fairing was designed and built before the model came to Europe.

Close scrutiny of the pictures will reveal that four Keihin carburetters breathe through cinder-boxes—rubber containers with wire mesh backing, which can hardly be called air-cleaners!

Ignition is by battery and coils, and the plugs, as on the works twins, are centrally located ; the cylinder-wall oiling via external pipes, which was used on some twins, does not appear to be employed on the four.

A dry multiple plate clutch is mentioned in the specification, but no details of the number of gears are given; fore and aft suspension is again similar to the twin; note the telescopic-type steering-damper used, probably as a result of Isle of Man experience.

250-c.c. HONDA FOUR

Four separate, flat-sided, Keihin carburetters are used; each pair is controlled by a 2-into-1 cable. Note the six-spring clutch carried well out in the open and the shaft and gear drive to the camshafts.

**An owned-from-new pre-war roadster
which is now a top-class racer**

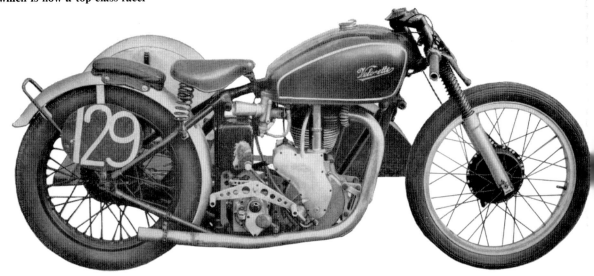

NO ONE CAN deny that North London sprint enthusiast, L. W. H. Collins, has had his money's worth out of the MSS Velocette which he purchased new in 1936 for £59 10s. Another bargain was the second-hand Watsonian sidecar which Len hitched to the machine twenty-three years ago.

At first the outfit was used with a touring-type sidecar body, for ride-to-work purposes. In this form it was raced by Len at Brooklands, where it won its class twice in tests over a flying kilometre—at speeds of about 65 m.p.h. During the war, it continued to do its

---

IN BRIEF

Engine: Single-cylinder, high-camshaft o.h.v.; 81-mm. bore × 96-mm. stroke = 495 c.c.; c.r. 10 : 1 : no performance figures available.
Fuel tank: Steel, 4-gal. capacity.
Oil tank: Steel, 4-pt. capacity.
Wheels: Light-alloy front rim with Dunlop 2·75-in. × 21-in. tyre; steel rear and sidecar rims with 3·25-in. × 19-in. and 3·00-in. × 19-in. Dunlop tyres respectively.

job as an everyday hack; since 1945 it has not been taxed for road use, but has been entered extensively for sprint runs. Until people started using Vincents, it was almost unbeaten in open sprints. And in its capacity class it is still almost unbeatable.

The original sidecar chassis, fitted with a light-alloy mudguard and a rather crude plank platform for the passenger, proved to be unnecessarily heavy and, in 1961, a lighter, more compact structure was fitted.

Considerably more work has been carried out on the Velocette. Following experiments with a compression ratio in the region of 14 : 1, the original engine burst and many replacement parts, including a crankcase, were fitted. An 'Al-Fin' barrel was obtained, but the original cast-iron head is still in residence, although it has been modified to take new valves—a Norton inlet and a Matchless exhaust. The former is larger than the MSS component, and the Matchless item has, to Len's way of thinking, a better shape.

A Martlett piston is carried on the

Timing side of the motor, showing the alloy carburetter trumpet and rocking pedal gearchange lever, both built by the owner.

This close-up of the 'works' clearly shows the alloy engine plates and extensive drilling.

original connecting-rod and big-end assembly—which must surely hold the record for longevity in a racing motor. Unusual in a racer is the absence of a rev.-counter. The B.T.H. magneto is set to provide its spark at 35° advance, for, in the owner's view, there is no time to tinker with ignition levers in a sprint!

Carburation is by a $\frac{5}{32}$-in.-bore Amal T.T. instrument with a home-built in-take funnel. Methanol is the fuel used, with 20/50 Viscostatic oil. Trans-mission is via the standard Velocette gearbox and clutch. The kick-starter has been removed and blanked off.

Also standard and original are the frame and wheels, but a pair of A.M.C. 'Teledraulic' front forks have been built in. The head crow lug is 'special' and a Webb steering-damper is used. A modi-fied front spindle has been made up for the Velocette front hub.

At the Brighton Speed Trials in 1954 the outfit was clocked at 96·4 m.p.h. at the end of the standing kilo. This equals 7,300 r.p.m. in top gear—the only accurate assessment of revolutions avail-able for the power unit.

100-b.h.p. contender for world's fastest solo title with J.A.P. '1,000' V-twin in an O.E.C.-Reynolds frame

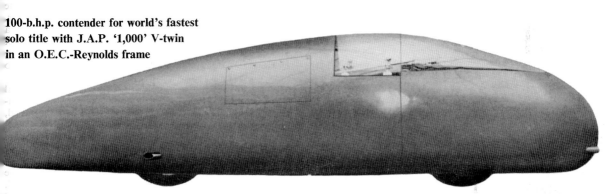

ENGLAND HAS A man and a machine all set to take a crack at the World Record Solo title, currently held since 1956 by NSU at 211 m.p.h. or Triumph at 214 m.p.h.—according to whether you believe the F.I.M. or the facts. Mancunian Bob Berry is the man, and the fully streamlined J.A.P.-engined monster which he has built over the past few years at his own expense is the machine.

Many people, hearing of Bob's effort when it was in the embryo stage, confidently predicted that he would never get it finished. He has, and it has run successfully at Pendine, South Wales, up to some 150 m.p.h. Now the Thomases are saying that it won't go fast enough. They point to the fate of earlier English expeditions, for it is over twenty years since an Englishman and machine last held the record (Eric Fernihough on a Brough Superior, April 19, 1937, 169·786 m.p.h.)

Bob Berry seated at the controls of his special.

Berry has been after the record before —with a Brough Superior, virtually unstreamlined, which proved disappointing in trials. His present design has been a long time in the building and the completed job shows several departures from the usual conception of a record machine.

Most startling, perhaps is the age and pattern of the frame. Basically, this is the O.E.C. component used by Joe Wright in 1930. It has been extensively modified so that the driver sits in front of the engine instead of over it, but the unorthodox O.E.C.-Duplex forks and steering assembly have been retained.

The front-wheel axle is carried on sliders controlled by springs inside a couple of almost upright tubes. These are connected to a further pair of tubes, which are actually part of the frame, by short links at top and bottom—rather like the links of girder forks, but pivoting on vertical axes. External Girling dampers have been fitted to the 30-year-old forks to give an improved action.

Both wheels specially built Dunlop tyres which have been safety-checked for speeds up to the 300-m.p.h. mark! There is at present no front brake, although one may be fitted later. The unsprung rear wheel, which has a brake, is carried in a pair of massive lugs at the frame-ends.

IN BRIEF

Engine: J.A.P. '8-80' o.h.v. 50° V-twin, 80-mm. bore × 99-mm. stroke = 996 c.c.; c.r. = 14·6 : 1 front, 14·2 : 1 rear; claimed output, 104 b.h.p at 6,800 r.p.m.
Fuel tank: 5-gal. light alloy.
Oil tank: 1-gal. light alloy.
Wheels: Steel rims carrying special Dunlop record-type tyres, 3·50 in. × 21 in. front and rear.
Weight: 640 lb.
Length overall: 181 in.
Maximum height: 40 in.
Maximum width: 22 in.
Wheelbase: 90 in.

Just astern of the seat a large windbox sits across the frame. This is connected to forward-facing twin tubes in the snout of the monster and feeds the intake sides of the 'track' Amal carburetters. Bob tells me it is calculated that he should gain 1 lb. sq. in. boost at 200 m.p.h. rising to a theoretical 2·2 lb. sq. in. at 300 m.p.h.

The engine is a modified '8–80' J.A.P. V-twin, with dual Lucas racing magnetos. Transmission is through a racing Norton four-speed gearbox, special Ferodo-lined clutch and Renold chain. The motor runs on an alcohol-base fuel and castor-base oil. Bob tells me that the present power output is 104 b.h.p.

On to the shell. Handsomely contoured, it was designed by Bob, who told that the shape came to him from watching a trout darting up-stream.

A framework was built of ½-in. steel tube and the shell was moulded-on by H.P. Pressurecast Ltd., of Manchester, resins and other materials being specially supplied by British Resin Products Ltd. It took four months to sand down the

shape once it had been made. The shell is in two pieces, bolted together just forward of the driver's seat.

Record-breaking upon private resources is a speculative business, and to attempt it needs some courage. I would like to wish the stocky Mancunian and his machine every success.

The massive O.E.C. duplex frame with rigid rear end has been modified by Reynolds Tubes to enable the driver to sit 'inside'. The hairpin-valve springs on the big J.A.P. are just visible here; a rev-counter drive is taken off the magneto bevel box.

21
BEART-PREPARED NORTON

**Production racer by famous
Guildford tuning-engineer**

IN STANDARD TRIM as it leaves the
factory the 'Manx' Norton looks a
beautifully prepared piece of racing
machinery, and it is difficult to convey
adequately in words the super-prepara-
tion that obviously goes into one of the
Beart-Nortons. I think the best sum-
mary of one of these models is to say
that it is a racer in *concours d'élégance*
condition!

An immediately obvious alteration
from standard is the adoption of green
as the basic machine colour. Francis
tells me that he has used this on all his
models since the war; one of its advantages is that the machine can be picked
out very easily in a bunch—a particularly useful asset when one is lap-scoring
on a crowded circuit.

LEFT: *A familiar figure at race tracks all over the country, Francis Beart fits a 'hard' plug to the '500' before the start of the Manx Grand Prix of 1960.*

RIGHT: *Rider Ellis Boyce had trouble with a sooting plug early during the 1960 M.G.P. Here he strives to make up time as he dashes through Creg-ny-Baa.*

The Beart-made clutch spring carrier plate is made of electron and incorporates a ball race for ease of operation.

Other alterations are less obvious, unless the machine is compared with similar models at the end of a race—when it will be found to have exuded very little oil as great attention has been paid to keeping oil inside, by means of extensive crankcase breathing. To this end small-bore pipes are taken from the front of the crankcase, the bottom bevel-cover and from just behind the drive shaft. Each has a de-frothing arrangement (trade secret!) inside its attachment union and the small pipes are led, alongside the two tank breathers, through a big-bore pipe terminating some 6 in. behind the seat. I saw the '500' just after it had completed the 1960 Senior Manx G.P. and all the pipe terminals were dry.

Changes in the engine are few. The drive-side main-bearing housing is altered, but otherwise the crankshaft/crankcase assembly is near standard, although the flywheel ensemble, as on all Beart models, is balanced to suit the individual frame. The combustion chamber shape is not altered and, although pistons are individually turned from forgings, they are made to a shape similar to standard. The port interiors are slightly changed. Valve timing is standard, as are the camshafts, but the cambox is freed-up considerably and the oil flow through the box is doubled. Special Terry valve springs are used with standard valves; carburetter is a 1⅜-in. Amal G.P.

The gearbox is as important on a racer as the engine and a lot of care is put into reassembling the standard box. The clutch is lightened by the adoption of an Elektron spring cover-plate which incorporates a ball race at its operating centre; bonded Ferodo linings are used. Clutch-spring boxes and the rear-wheel sprocket are turned from Dural. When the engine and box are fitted to the frame, the lower rear crankcase/engine-plate bolt is dispensed with and the plates cut back to suit. This means that the gearbox can be removed without disturbing the engine. The heads

IN BRIEF

Engine: Norton single-cylinder d.o.h.c.; light-alloy barrel and head; 86-mm. bore × 85·6 mm. stroke = 499 c.c.; 11·3 : 1 c.r.; peak r.p.m. 7,400.
Transmission: Four-speed A.M.C. gearbox.
Fuel: 4-gal. 6½-pt. light-alloy tank.
Oil: 6-pt. in a 1-gal. light-alloy tank.
Wheels: Light-alloy rims with Avon racing tyres, 3·00 in. × 19 in. front, 3·50 in. × 19 in. rear.

of all the bolts have been lightened—a tedious business, but it saves weight.

The standard 'Featherbed' frame is also lightened slightly and the rear engine attachment cross-tube is brazed *in situ* instead of being bolted up. A lighter fork top clip and crown and column are used and the fork-damping is modified from standard. Special foot-rests are used which have integral nuts, enabling them to be spanner-tightened. Other lightness-makers used by Francis include alloy spoke nipples and Elektron rear-wheel spacers. Both hubs are machined all over and weight-reduced and the front drum has extra large diameter fins shrunk-on to give optimum anti-fade properties. The standard oil tank is used, but is fitted on dowels via rubber bushes instead of the through-bolt fixing. Petrol tanks are specially made by Wakefield's of Byfleet in light alloy.

Jubilee clips are used to position the glass-fibre rear mudguard. Note the carburetter bellmouth and the lightening of bolt heads and frame gussets.

79

The A.J.S. 500-c.c. twin used by the factory team in the 1954 T.T.

NINETEEN-FIFTY-FOUR was destined to be a memorable year, for it was to see the end of British factory teams in the Senior T.T. and, come to that, in international road racing generally. At the end of that season the 'production model only' rule came into operation so far as they were concerned.

The 1954 A.J.S. racers were lineal descendants of the original 'Porcupines' and were ridden in that year's 'Senior' by Rod Coleman, Derek Farrant and Bob McIntyre.

You may recall that in 1954 conditions were appalling and the race was stopped after four laps. It had stopped at Quarter Bridge on lap one for Farrant as he dropped the plot in the rain. Coleman had held fifth place for the first three laps, but then retired at the pit with a split fuel tank and McIntyre eventually brought the other twin home in fourteenth place. Better luck came their way in the Ulster Grand Prix, a few weeks later, when Rod Coleman came in second, only half a minute astern of the late Ray Amm's Norton. This race, like the T.T., was run in foul weather conditions and was shortened to just over half its intended distance.

It is fair to say that the 'Porcupine' is different from any other British Senior racer. It has unit construction of engine and gearbox and gear primary drive with the engine running 'backwards'. The engine is near enough 'square'

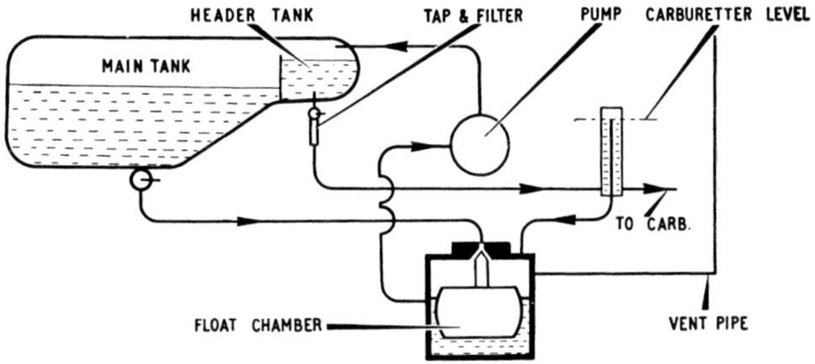

This diagram shows how the complicated petrol supply system operated.

IN BRIEF

Engine: A.J.S. d.o.h.c. parallel-twin inclined at 45°; light-alloy barrel and heads; 68-mm. bore $\times$ 68·25-mm. stroke = 499 c.c.; 54 b.h.p. at 7,500 r.p.m.

Transmission: Gear primary drive to four-speed gearbox in unit with engine.

Fuel: 6½-gal. light-alloy tank.

Oil: 7-pt. sump.

Wheels: Light-alloy rims carrying Dunlop racing tyres, 3·00 in. $\times$ 19 in. front, 3·50 in. $\times$ 19 in. rear.

Wheelbase: 56½ in.

Weight: 335 lb. approx.

dimensionally and has a 'Y' gear-train to drive the twin camshafts, although the magneto, a Lucas rotating-magnet instrument, is driven by a short chain. Obviously, light alloy is used throughout, including the large oil sump, which holds castor-base lubricant. The barrels and heads are inclined at 45° to the horizontal and the twin G.P. carburetters of 1⅛-in. choke size, have an extra 4° of downdraught. They are individually carried on rubber inlet pipes, so that they are relatively unaffected by vibration. The fuel-feed system is unusual in that a weir replaces the normal float

chamber. As can be seen, by reference to the diagram, fuel flows from the main tank to a float chamber situated to the rear of the gearbox. From there it goes via a pump driven from the magneto drive cross-shaft to a header tank inside the main tank, and then it is fed by gravity to the weir, which is set for level in the same manner as a normal float chamber. Fuel then goes to the carburetters and surplus passes over the weir back to the float chamber. To prime the system the model has to be stood nearly vertically on its rear wheel to get fuel over the barrier between the header

and main tank, which operation used to cause a certain amount of mirth among the riders!

Similarity to the production A.M.C. twins is noticeable in the employment of plain centre-main and big-end bearings. Roller journals are used for the outer mains.

Major innovations were made to the frame of the E.95—to give the model its prosaic factory designation—for 1953, when a loop type was introduced instead of the open one previously used. For 1954 the new frame was lowered about $1\frac{1}{2}$ in. and a massive $6\frac{1}{2}$-gal. alloy tank was draped around to enclose the motor and provide a high degree of streamlining without extra charge!

The all-welded frame has its swinging fork controlled by the now obsolete A.M.C. 'jam-pot' units. Front forks are a racing edition of the famous Teledraulics which have been an A.M.C. feature for almost 20 years.

Close-up, showing the float chamber just astern of the sump.

Alcohol-burning 100 b.h.p.
big-twin

Driving side: note the batteries carried between the engine plates at front and rear.

IN BRIEF

Engine: J.A.P. 50° o.h.v. Vee-twin; 80-mm. bore × 99-mm. stroke = 994 c.c.; c.r. 14 : 1; approx. 95 b.h.p. at 6,500–7,000 r.p.m.
Fuel: 3½-gal. light-alloy tank.
Oil: ½ gal. in 1-gal. light-alloy tank.
Ignition: Lucas coils and distributors, Varley 12 v. battery.
Wheels: Light alloy rims carrying Avon racing tyres, 4·00 in. × 18 in. rear; 3·00 in. × 19 in. front.
Wheelbase: 56½ in.

84

BIG-TWINS HAVE a special attraction. The very design of the engine suggests bags of power—lusty power. And when the unit ticks over, whether it is an antique sidevalve or a new racing machine, its beefy bangs assert their authority much more than the rasp of a 'four' could ever do. Francis Williams's Norton-J.A.P. comes within the racing (rather than the antique) category, for it has almost everything a sprint rider could wish for. Good steering is assured by the 'Featherbed' frame, forks and wheels, and an abundance of power is on tap from the extensively modified racing J.A.P. engine.

This model is the second big-twin of its type that Frank has built.

A 1952–54 long-stroke 350-c.c. Norton 'Manx' provided the cycle parts of the machine. Apart from welding on extra lugs to carry additional engine fixing bolts just in front of and just behind the crankcase base, and replacing the swinging fork spindle with one of ⅝-in. diameter running in metal bushes, instead of the original Silentblocs, the frame is as original. It has been satin-chrome-

plated to provide an unchippable finish. The front forks have been cleaned up, but they, too, are pretty well standard, as are the conical hubs with single leading-shoe brakes both fore and aft. An 18-in. rim has been built on to the rear hub to take a very special Avon sprint tyre. One look at the tread shows that it is intended for straight-ahead use only!

Transmission is by Perry chains via a pre-'Featherbed' type 'Manx' Norton box. The clutch has been made into a five-plate type and the sprocket has a bonded-on Ferodo lining in place of the usual inserts. A top gear of about 3½ : 1 is used on a kilometre sprint, so Francis tells me. Terminal velocity at the end of this distance is about 150 m.p.h.!

The engine is very different from other sprint 1,000-c.c. J.A.P. units. It has a crankcase of the type employed on 1,100-c.c. racing cars, which is much sturdier than the 8/80 one. The driving-side main bearing uses one roller and one ball journal; on the timing side a Dural cage carries two rows of ¼-in. by ¼-in. rounded-edge rollers which run direct on the mainshaft. This is an F.J.W.

modification, as the original rollers were $\frac{1}{2}$ in. by $\frac{1}{4}$ in. The big-end has a double row of $\frac{1}{4}$ in. by $\frac{1}{4}$ in. rollers in the forked (front) connecting rod and needle rollers in the single rod.

Hepolite pistons giving 14 : 1 compression ratio run in Wellworthy 'Al-Fin' barrels. The silver-painted cylinder heads are made of cast-ron material and have been cut to accommodate larger inlet and exhaust valves, both made of KE965 steel, and a second 14-mm. sparking plug which screws in between the push-rod covers. Apart from double hairpin valve springs, each rocker has its individual return spring, and each push-rod cover tube contains a push-rod return spring in its bottom section.

Lubrication is of the dry sump principle by gear pumps carried immediately under the timing-chest. Castor-base oil is used and a bleed is taken from the delivery side of the pump to the rear base of the front pot.

Two Amal GP carburetters are used; of $1\frac{1}{4}$-in. choke size they are carried on extension pieces to give slightly longer inlet tracts. The float

chambers are carried remotely and are mounted at top and bottom in rubber diaphragms.

Ignition is by twin coils and distributors. These latter are bevel-driven from the timing side of the engine and have Lucas caps and modified internals on 'F.J.W.' bodies. The shafts run on pin-bearings and only the rear distributor has a contact-breaker in it. This actuates the twin coils in series, each feeds one distributor and either distributor feeds two plugs, one in each pot. Frank tells me that use of one contact-breaker eliminates the impossible job of synchronizing a pair! The system is 12-volt and relies on six 2-volt Varley cells connected in series.

Timing side: the two distributors are bevel driven and each feeds one plug in each cylinder.

Hybrid cross-country model

IT IS PROBABLE that Triumph engines have been used in more specials than have any other make, but most of these specials employed either a Norton or a home-brewed frame. This machine, owned by Southend dealer Peter Watkin in 1961, used a frame originally intended for a '250'—a cast-alloy-beam-type Greeves.

One of the unit-construction Triumph power-plants, with four-speed gearbox, forms the basis of the model. But it has not been a case of just finding an engine and popping it into a frame.

The unit started life as a 5TA (500-c.c. 'Speed Twin') and it was originally built-up for scrambling with a 3TA (350-c.c. 'Twenty-one') barrel and head. After the machine had proved itself a practical proposition, the motor was reassembled with the 500-c.c. barrel and T100A (500-c.c. 'Tiger 100') pistons, which give a ratio of 10·5 : 1, because the '350' head has been retained. The head's inlet tract has been opened out to take the 1-in. Amal 'Monobloc' carburetter from the 5TA engine.

The motor is standard so far as mains, big-ends and valve timing are concerned.

A home-built air cleaner, using an assembly of nylon pot-scourers as an element, actually gives two-stage cleaning, because the air passes through a primary chamber which allows some of the heavier dust particles to 'settle out' before the cleaner section is reached.

The energy-transfer ignition at present employed consists of T100A parts. The ignition is fixed (an auto-advance is standard), which arrangement has proved satisfactory, but Peter has plans to try the coil-and-battery again which he had previously experimented with. B.T.H. racing platinum points are used on the standard contact-breaker to eliminate 'burning' troubles.

Light alloy, to RM70 specification and $\frac{1}{4}$ in. thick, is employed for the engine mounting plates, which sweep deeply under the unit so that five bolts, with distance pieces, can be fitted between them. This makes the plates into what is virtually an H section girder, with consequent increase in strength—and, incidentally, provides a substantial 'crankcase shield' for rough rockeries.

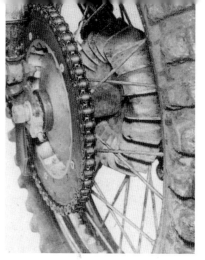

Rear hub in close-up, with the $\frac{1}{4}$-in. wide sprocket and $\frac{3}{8}$-in. chain that gives extra self-aligning properties.

The 5TA unit is a really snug fit into the Greeves frame. Both engine plates are extra deep so as to permit cross bracing between them for increased rigidity.

The cycle parts are mainly standard Greeves scrambler components. To cope with the extra weight, Girling rear units from a B.S.A. 'Gold Star', fitted with springs of 110-lb. rating are used, and the rubber-in-torsion units at the front have been given more preloading than in the original '250'. But the main components, forks, frame and wheels have not been altered.

A Triumph 4¼-pt. oil tank is mounted on the offside and the breather from this is fed into the swinging fork so that the oil eventually blows out on to the rear chain through the standard Greeves oiler.

In order to lower the gear ratios, the teeth were turned off the Triumph final-drive sprocket, a B.S.A. sprocket was bored and then the two were welded together.

A box has been welded into the bottom of the Greeves tank to act as a coil container and also to clear the tops of the rocker-boxes. No steadying bracket is fitted to the cylinder head and none is required. Just to help the hybridization process, Peter has fitted a pair of ex-works A.M.C. handlebars!

The complete machine weighs only 280 lb., 50 more than the 250-c.c. Greeves scrambler.

IN BRIEF

Engine: Triumph parallel-twin o.h.v.; light-alloy cylinder head; cast-iron barrel; 69-mm. bore × 65·5-mm. stroke = 490 c.c.; 10·5 : 1 c.r. No b.h.p. figures available.

Transmission: Four-speed gearbox in unit with engine.

Fuel: 1¼-gal. steel tank.

Oil: 4¼-pt. steel tank.

Wheels: Steel rims carrying Dunlop Sports tyres, 3·00 in. × 21 in. front, 4·00 in. × 19 in. rear; 6-in. brakes front and rear.

Wheelbase: 52 in.

Weight: 280 lb.